PERSPECTIVES

PERSPECTIVES

A Collection of Devotions

Looking at Life Through the Lens of Christ

Tom Sperry

EQUIP PRESS

Colorado Springs

PERSPECTIVES

Published by Equip Press, Colorado Springs, CO

First Edition: 2021
Perspectives / Tom Sperry
Paperback ISBN: 978-1-951304-74-4
eBook ISBN: 978-1-951304-75-1
Library of Congress Control Number: 2021914937

Dedicated to my wonderful wife Debbi,
My children Jennifer and Douglas,
And my grandsons Jackson, Austin, Mason, and Tyler

We all have many options regarding how we look at life. Choosing to look at life through the lens of Christ offers real peace, joy, and confidence in our loving God. We have the choice to approach life with Christ-like purpose and Christ-like attitudes. See clearly and compassionately through the lens of Christ.

I have written these devotions over the past twenty years with the hope that they might encourage the reader. The thoughts are my own and are not meant to represent any particular denomination or dogma. All biblical references are from The Jerusalem Bible unless noted. I have found this translation to be very readable and easy to understand. I have substituted the word God for Yahweh as a personal preference.

I am a retired pharmacist, having practiced pharmacy for 38 years with a BS degree in pharmacy from the University of the Pacific. In 2018 I earned a bachelor of theology degree from Northwestern Theological Seminary and have been involved in developing a school chaplaincy program for elementary age children. Writing these devotions has helped me with my faith, and I pray that the reader may find some devotions that are helpful and an encouragement.

IN THE BEGINNING

"In the beginning, God created the heavens and the earth."

GENESIS 1:1

This simple verse is the foundation for all of our faith. Without acknowledging God as our creator, there can be no faith. Without God at our center, we have no soul, no redemption. Eternal life would be a myth. Without God as our creator, there is no hope.

By acknowledging God as our creator, our whole world as a living soul is opened to us. God gives us everything—a soul, hope, redemption, love, and purpose. We have been made in His image; we are capable of emotion, trust, and faith. How precious it is to acknowledge God as our creator. God is our beginning. God's hand is in us. How blessed we are.

As we go day by day through this coming year we can live with joy and comfort knowing that we are a created being, formed by the hand of God. We can enjoy His gifts and grace. We have been given the ability to know right from wrong. We have the capability to show compassion, to love, to realize that there is more to us than mere flesh and blood. We are living souls, placed here for a purpose, God's purpose.

Do you live each day as a created child of God? Do you recognize your special nature? Will you utilize the precious gift of life for the honor of God?

Commit yourself to daily prayer and praise. You are God's creation. Keep God in you as you are in God. Live as God has created you, in faith, trust and joy.

"The fear of God is the beginning of knowledge;
Fools spurn wisdom and discipline."

PROVERBS 1:7

FIRST OF ALL

"My advice is that, first of all, there should be prayers offered for everyone—petitions, intercessions, and thanksgiving—and especially for kings and others in authority, so that we may be able to live religious and reverent lives in peace and quiet."

1 TIMOTHY 2:1

First of all: prayer. Prayer for everyone. It is easy to bring our own concerns and our concerns for those that we love before God. How often do we pray for those who have authority over us? How often do we pray for our enemies? We all have persons who have some authority over us and this verse instructs us to pray for them.

Prayer has power and God can do miracles. We know that God wants all to be saved and we should do everything we can to glorify God with our attitude and love toward everyone. Lifting up everyone in prayer puts us in an attitude of peace and harmony before God. Do our actions and attitudes toward others get in the way of their salvation? Is God revealed through you?

How different our attitude toward others would be if we spent time praying for them! We need to be concerned for everyone. Our prayers have power! Pray with thanksgiving for the blessings we all enjoy. Pray for godly intercession for all those in need. Pray that the hearts of the ungodly would be open for the Holy Spirit.

Through prayer we acknowledge where the power to affect lives lies. It is with God. Prayer is an important part of our personal walk with God. It keeps our eyes focused on Him. So, first of all...pray!

"A man's pride brings him humiliation,
he who humbles himself will win honor."

PROVERBS 29:23

TO PRAY

"Now it was about this time that He went out into the hills to pray; and He spent the whole night in prayer to God."

LUKE 6:12

If you are like me, time seems to be going by faster and faster. Setting aside time for the important things grows increasingly difficult as I am overwhelmed by an avalanche of information. Life throws at me more things to buy, more information to consume, and more "experts" that want to share how to make my life better. How can I make time for God? Is God relevant to me?

What a great example we have in Jesus. He found the time. He committed His attention to be alone with the Father. He was intimate with the Father. He prayed.

Without prayer, it is too easy to lose track of Jesus. Overwhelmed by the demands of day-to-day life, it is too easy to only call on God on my schedule, if there is time left over. Too often my prayer is reserved for either asking for something I need or letting God know how I think things should be going. Too often I do not hold on to an intimate relationship with Him. Too often I forget to give Him the praise and honor and thanks that He deserves. Too often I fail.

I need to remember that God first loved me. He gives, He saves, He loves. He is active. Despite my shortcomings and despite my sins He continues to love me and is there for me…always. He created me for a relationship, yet too often I do not keep up my end of the bargain. I am selfish and self-serving, leaving my misguided perception that God is a glorified ATM machine, meant to serve me and answer my prayers on demand. I expect God to answer me on my terms and turn to Him on a need's basis only. I fail time and time again.

But Jesus reminds me that prayer is a life-giving conduit to God. It is through prayer that I know that God is in charge. Prayer makes God personal. Prayer makes God real. Prayer changes me. Too often I forget to be thankful…for the big and small things…for life and faith. Too often I push God away and forget the strength and wisdom that are His. Too often I forget how powerful and loving God is. Too often I forget the freedom and peace that He can provide. Too often.

So today I commit to follow the example of Jesus. I commit to go and pray for however long it takes to rest in the intimate love of the Father. I commit to thanking Him. I commit to recognizing Him. I commit to loving Him. I hope you will join me.

"The sacrifice of the wicked is abhorrent to God,
Dear to Him is the prayer of honest men."

PROVERBS 15:8

A SIMPLE YES

"All you need to say is "Yes" if you mean yes, "No" if you mean no; anything more than this comes from the evil one."

MATTHEW 5:37

Today's society demands shades of gray, pursuing a course of relativism and rationalization. Absolute truth is pushed aside as we try to feel good about poor decisions we have made and frame the truth into our own fashion. What a dangerous path we are on! Truth and honesty are not situational.

There is absolute truth. God's love for us is absolute truth, yet too often we fail to mirror His love. Too often our love for God is determined by events, not our heart. God's promises to us are absolute truth, yet too often we want instant answers and instant gratification.

Through Christ's sacrifice on the cross, God is completely and eternally committed to us. This is absolute truth, yet too often we shy away from chances to witness for Him. Too often we seek God only because of our needs as we see them.

Honesty and transparency are more than just high ideals; they are our duty as followers of Christ. Our actions and lives should reveal openness and candor, never ambivalence or secretiveness. Half-truths are becoming more accepted all the time. They are a path to destruction, allowing us to convince ourselves that truth is something that can be shaded in our favor. When God looks at our hearts there are no half-truths. The mind may make excuses and condone partial truth, but the heart knows the meaning of this verse. Our conscience knows that despite the personal ramifications, clarity and truth should prevail.

Too often we feel our decisions require explanation to justify our position. It is either right or wrong as a Christian, self-serving or sacrificial as a Christian, situational half-truth or absolute truth. A Christian's word must be trustworthy and dependable. Our yes must mean yes always, and our no must mean no always. This type of response shows our dedication and commitment to honesty, truth, and clarity. Make sure you stand for what you say.

"The contrary heart does not find happiness,
The deceitful tongue falls into distress."

PROVERBS 17:20

ONLY JESUS

"Jesus said: 'I am the Way, the Truth and the Life. No one can come to the Father except through Me.'"

JOHN 14:6

We want to keep our options open. We want to have choices in life. We want to feel like we have some sort of control of our future. The truth is there is only one option, one choice, and one future: Jesus Christ. He is the pure embodiment of the entire plan for our salvation and relationship with the Father. Jesus and Jesus alone. There are no exceptions, carve-outs, or waivers. There is no special treatment because of your status or finances. Jesus offers the same promise, the same reality, and the same pathway to everyone.

Religion is not the way to the Father. Sacrifice, rites, and piety do not get us to heaven. There is no liturgy that can be recited and no repetitious prayer that is the replacement for Jesus. Jesus is the only way. Not just the knowledge of Jesus, but the true, real person of a powerful, loving Jesus that we know personally. Our path to the Father is not a roadmap of waypoints of accomplishments. Faith in Jesus is the road. Acknowledging Him as our Savior is our compass. His sacrificial atonement for our sins is our conduit to an eternity with Him. Doing our best to live a life closer and closer to the example of Jesus is our happy obligation. There is no other way. Let Him lead the way.

In a time when the world seems to be in turmoil, one of the things that is missing the most is truth. We all want our own truth as we see it and as we remember it through a cloudy lens. Absolute truth gives way to relative truth. We use our truth as a tool to make a point or try to influence others. When we do not know truth we cannot trust. The good news is Jesus is the absolute truth. He is one person we can trust completely. The only motive of Jesus is to follow the will of the Father and to be the path and means to our salvation. When He speaks it is pure truth, absolute and unchanging. Truth is part of His character and He can be depended upon always. God is love and Jesus proves that truth.

Real life comes with the freedom in Jesus through faith. From faith comes fruit and the ability to live life to its fullest in its purest form. Love comes from Jesus. Peace, joy, and patience are only obtainable through Jesus. Sin cannot take those attributes away from Jesus. He is life. He is power. He is peace. He is love.

We as a society struggle with control. We want to make decisions for others and be in charge of our own lives. We want to fix things our way, for ourselves. We plan, we maneuver, we try to get an advantage. Jesus asks you to give in to Him and identify with His sacrifice which He performed for each of us. We are not good at obedience, yet that is what is required. We want the glory for ourselves, yet glorifying God is what is needed. We think we earn everything we have, yet thanking God for His provision is the mind of a believer. Our way will fail every time, yet the way of Jesus has already won. He IS the ONLY WAY, He IS the only absolute TRUTH, and He is the fullness of LIFE eternal. Faith in Jesus lets us join with Him in His victory. Faith in Jesus lets us share in His nature of truth and life. Faith in Jesus gives us the hope and joy that He intends for each of us. Jesus and only Jesus.

"God guides a man's steps:
How could man discern the way he goes?"

PROVERBS 20:24

REJOICE

"Rejoice in the Lord always. I will say it again, Rejoice!"

PHILIPPIANS 4:4

Do you live your life rejoicing in the Lord? Can anybody tell? The life of a Christian is pure joy, yet so much of our time is spent worrying and in sadness. Rejoice is a very active word. It is more than just being happy with an occasional smile. Rejoice! It is an attitude and lifestyle. It is a way of life. It is embracing your joy with thanksgiving for the gifts we have been given by God. It is looking for opportunities to give praise. It is living our lives with freedom, peace, and joy. It is trusting God to see us through all circumstances and acknowledging that we cannot do everything ourselves.

We don't rejoice because of our Lord, we rejoice in Him, filled with His Spirit. We celebrate in the Lord, as part of Him, the undeserving beneficiaries of His blessings and sacrifices. We are told to rejoice always. It is so easy to forget the gifts of God when things aren't going as we have planned or problems arise.

We are not promised a problem-free life, nor should we expect one. On the contrary, problems will be put before us to help us mature in Christ. We need to know that we may be limited to solve problems, but God is not!

What a great reason to rejoice. Our Lord is a living Lord, working all things for good to those who believe in Him.

The promises of God are real and we are the recipients of His grace, not for a short while, but for all eternity. Look at your attitude today. Commit yourself to rejoicing—at all times.

"For the sorrowing every day is evil,
for the joyous heart it is festival always."

PROVERBS 15:15

PSALM 23

"God is my shepherd, I lack nothing.
In meadows of green grass He lets me lie.
To the waters of repose He leads me;
There He revives my soul.
He guides me by paths of virtue
For the sake of His name.
Though I pass through a gloomy valley, I fear no harm;
Beside me Your rod and Your staff are there to hearten me.
You prepare a table before me under the eyes of my enemies;
You anoint my head with oil, my cup brims over.
Ah, how goodness and kindness pursue me,
Every day of my life;
My home, the house of God,
As long as I live."

MY PERSPECTIVES

GOD'S TIMING

"Keep yourselves within the love of God and wait for the mercy of our Lord Jesus Christ to give you eternal life."

JUDE 21

God's timing is always perfect and purposeful. As much as we might like it to be different, we are not in charge of when and how God works in our lives. When we keep ourselves within the love of God we can live without fear and without deadline. We live with a fullness of expectation. Our call is to remain, holding fast to Christ and relying on His strength to see us through. With all the pressures of the world it is easy to lose sight of His strength and begin depending upon ourselves and our agenda. We have become an obsessed society in regards to time. We want things faster and faster, letting short-term goals overshadow the value of patience and peace. We must always remind ourselves that God is in control of circumstance and time. He never fails. He never hurries. He is always right. Be patient and keep yourself under His authority and His love.

Waiting is not something that we do well. We worry. We fret. We want to be in control.

Providing is something God does perfectly. We need not worry. We need not be anxious. God is in control.

Instead, remain in love. Wait on the Lord as he will provide the right thing at the right time for eternal good. Trust Him and let God be God.

"He stands guard over the paths of justice,
He keeps watch on the way of His devoted ones."

PROVERBS 2:8

CALLED TO BE FREE

"My brothers, you were called, as you know, to liberty; but be careful, or this liberty will provide an opening for self-indulgence."

GALATIANS 5:13

What does it really mean to live free? Does it mean you are free to live an unencumbered life, focused on your own personal pleasure? Or does it mean much, much more? Could it be that God provided your freedom to be His agent of love and mercy in a world crying out for compassion? Could it be that your freedom serves to change the focus on what is required in the flesh to what is right in the Spirit? Could it be that without manmade restraint and expectations, we are all free to live bold, confident lives in humbleness to God? Where is your focus? On the bodily self or spiritual God?

Paul was telling the followers of Christ that no human dictate and no human set of rules can get in the way of the power of the Spirit. Everyone would be held bondage to the Law without the saving grace of Christ. The choice was simple: slavery in sin, or liberty in Christ.

The warning comes in the confusion of what being free really means. Christ's freedom is the unleashing of one's ability to love. Nothing holds us back from reflecting Christ. The same freedom does not say that since

I am free I can do anything I want with no repercussions. On the contrary, freedom means we can look away from ourselves and toward others in a spirit of love to do the work that Christ has put in front of us. There is freedom in sacrifice for Christ. There is freedom in humility for Christ. There is freedom in service to the Almighty God. Live free!

The soul of a Christian can never be repressed by sets of rules. He is controlled by a much higher calling, a calling to live a life of love in Christ. While man tries to control behavior, there is no controlling the power of the Spirit in man. Can you ever live up to the Law? NO. Can you ever find peace in restriction? NO. Can anything hold you back when Christ lives in you? NO. Can you feel the burden lifted when you rely on God and not yourself? YES.

Confidence, joy, contentment, humility, service, and peace are but a few things that await a believer who is liberated by Christ. Regulation can never come between God and us. We are always free to love, free to show compassion, and free to serve our Lord. Live free!

"The godless is forever coveting,
The virtuous man gives without ever refusing."

PROVERBS 21:26

DO WHAT IS RIGHT

"Everyone who knows what is the right thing to do and doesn't do it commits a sin."

JAMES 4:17

How do we determine the right thing to do? It doesn't have anything to do with interpretation or technicalities of the law. It doesn't have anything to do with status or circumstances. God has given each of us a conscience, an inward knowledge to discern right from wrong.

Somehow we seem to think that the line between right and wrong can become blurred and we can rationalize an incorrect action. Look at circumstances through pure eyes. Life would be so much simpler and so much more honorable if we would simply do what is right.

Selfishness and self-importance cloud our judgment. We need to set aside personal elevation and greed to see how we fit into God's plan and do what is right in the eyes of the Lord. Too many times we act on our version of the truth, one which gives us personal advantage. Too often we put the desires of people of influence above those with limited advantage to us. We do things to get ourselves ahead or attempt to accumulate future influence.

A clear conscience is a blessing! Knowing we have done what is fair to all concerned brings harmony and peace. God has provided the gift of discernment. Examining your heart and taking the time to listen to God will let you know what is the right thing to do.

Do you live your life striving to do what is right? Do you treat those you work with fairly? Do you find contentment in helping others succeed, or does pride and prestige hinder your relationships? Do you see humbleness as weakness, or does your joy come from knowing that you are fulfilling your commitment to a life in Christ?

Examine your heart and see if your motives and actions reveal your acceptance of what is the right thing to do. When you are faced with any decision the course of action is simple. Do the right thing.

"I have educated you in the ways of wisdom,
I have guided you along the paths of honesty."

PROVERBS 4:11

UNVEILED FACES

"And we, with our unveiled faces reflecting like mirrors the brightness of the Lord, all grow brighter and brighter as we are turned into the image that we reflect; this is the work of the Lord who is Spirit."

2 CORINTHIANS 3:18

Transparency. It is so honest, but is so hard to do. We all want to keep part of ourselves hidden from others, ourselves, and God. There seems to always be a thin barrier between being completely open with God and not trusting Him to see through our flaws, loving us all the while, regardless of our commitment to Him. We hold back, knowing there are parts of ourselves that feel unworthy and guilty. We all have a veil that is unique to us that alone we cannot remove. By ourselves, we can never be truly transparent. We need Jesus.

The work of the Spirit of the Lord is the path to freedom for our hearts and souls. If we can remove our masks long enough to see the brightness of the Lord we can let our lives take on new meaning, new excitement, and new energy. Removing the mask that keeps us from the brightness is liberating. There is no need to hide, no need to be guilty, and no need to regret. When we are truly transparent nothing blurs the image of God. We see Him more and more clearly as our spirit grows brighter and brighter in the Lord. Hiding part of ourselves is hard work and totally unnecessary. Being open to the brightness of the Lord is uplifting and transforming. The work of the Lord in our lives can change everything. We need Jesus.

The goal of the believer is to grow closer and closer to the image of God. We need to recognize what stands in the way of our full commitment to Him and remove those barriers. We need to know that the power of the Spirit is more powerful and transformational than anything we can do by ourselves. We need to be open and honest as we feel and experience His power in our lives. We must feel His brightness in every phase of our lives, and then reflect that brightness to do His will. His love toward us, reflected through us to others, can do amazing things. The more open we are with Jesus, the more mature we become in our faith. We can be beacons of light and hope, love and compassion, and obedience and thanksgiving when we let the Spirit reign in our hearts. We need Jesus.

Take off the veil. Let everyone see you for who you are...a saved child of God.

"The path of the virtuous is like the light of dawn,
Its brightness growing to the fullness of day."

PROVERBS 4:18

SEE GOD IN EVERYTHING

"Ever since God created the world, His everlasting power and deity—however invisible—have been there for the mind to see in the things He has made."

ROMANS 1:20

Look around you. Don't just see, but look. What a glorious creation God has made! We live in the midst of the greatest gift of all and are allowed to experience a full life, surrounded by the miracles of God. God has created all things for us! The songs of the birds of the air, the freshness of the ocean breeze, the shadows of the mighty mountains, the soul that dwells within us all shout out that God is real.

God is many things, but this verse reminds us of two very important truths. God is power. God is deity. We are not an accident, nor is the magnificent world in which we live. Celebrate God's power and deity! Enjoy and cherish all its magnificence! Take joy in nature. It is your gift. Appreciate and tend after your environment. It is your gift. Who can deny God when you see nature revealed in all its glory?

Just as God works invisibly in your heart, He invisibly created this world and everything in it. It all has purpose, just as each and every one of us does. The world around us is a continual reminder that God is God. He is beyond our comprehension. He is God! God is not just a theory or someone to pray to when things aren't going well. God and His creation are with us each and every day.

As awesome as His power and deity are, this verse tells us one more important fact. God is everlasting. What comfort and excitement this should give us. God is power, God is God, and He is forever. He had a plan for everything and every person that He created. We are each created with the same intricate care as all of nature. Take time to see the glory found in His creations, both in nature and in us. Let the mountains and valleys shout the reality of the power of God. You are as important a creation as any part of nature. Let yourself also shout the reality of the power of God. Live as God intends you to, part of His plan, part of His creation.

"God guides man's steps:
how could man discern the way he goes?"

PROVERBS 20:24

UNDO

"It was to undo all that the devil has done that the Son of God appeared."

1 JOHN 3:8

Hit the undo button. Clear your browser history. Erase your website activity. Check your security settings. Need to refresh your screen? We all have things in our lives that we wish we could erase, forget, or pretend never happened. We all have things we regret and feel some guilt about. Like it or not, the devil has had a hand in parts of our lives. Without the Son of God we are victims, but with Him we are victors. Hold on to Jesus.

With Jesus our chaos can become calm, our storms can become peace, and our selfishness can become generosity. The work of the devil, our sin, has been undone by Jesus. Our lost souls have been won through Him, and we can claim righteousness through faith in Him and His grace. A lost world has been saved. The power of the devil has been undone by the power of the Almighty God. God has always had a plan for our salvation, and it came in the person of Jesus Christ. Our sinful nature is overwhelmed by the grace of God. Our failings never get in the way of the love of God. The light of Christ has undone the darkness of the devil. Never forget that God has more power, more love, and more grace than the devil could ever pretend to have. With

Christ, we are victorious even when we fall short, full of joy even in hard circumstances, and assured of His mercy even when we do not deserve it.

There is great comfort when we know that God never gives up on us. We sin and doubt, but the love of God is never far away. He forgives and strengthens because He is love. He undoes our doubt with His ever-present grace. As I confess, He undoes my sin with His mercy. Even as we sometimes drift, He never leaves us alone. He is God. The only God. His mercy and grace have undone the power of the devil forever. We can rest peacefully, assured of Christ's undoing of everything the devil has done.

Feel like you need a reset? Look to Jesus. Feel like you need a new direction? Jesus is the way. Ever feel powerless? The power of Christ renews us constantly. In Christ we are refreshed and new creatures. Let Him undo the work of the devil in your life. The freedom that Christ gives is waiting.

"For the errors of the ignorant lead to their death,
and the complacency of fools works their own ruin;
but whoever listens to me may live secure,
he will have quiet, fearing no mischance."

PROVERBS 1:32-33

PSALM 103

Verses 8-12

"God is tender and compassionate,
Slow to anger, most loving;
His indignation does not last forever,
His resentment exists a short time only;
He never treats us, never punishes us,
As our guilt and our sins deserve.
No less than the height of heaven over earth
Is the greatness of His love for those who fear him;
He takes our sins farther away
Than the east is from the west."

MY PERSPECTIVES

TODAY

"Every day, as long as this 'today' lasts, keep encouraging one another so that none of you is hardened by the lure of sin."

HEBREWS 3:13

Isn't it hard to live in the present? How much time is spent pondering the past and worrying about the future? It is so easy to let old guilt and tomorrow's fear get in the way of living with a soft heart. Every day is a new day, full of new challenges, problems, and possibilities. Our lives can change in an instant, but our eternity is secure. We are one phone call, a diagnosis, or an accident away from turning our lives upside down, yet the love of Christ never changes. We plan, stress, and worry, yet we are held in the hands of a loving God. How can we look at things through the lens of Christ instead of the lens of the world? Only through faith.

It seems like the way the world is headed only further drives people apart and alienates us. In a "me first" time, we see demands, anger, and selfishness on the rise. This moment in time begs for more listening, more understanding, and more empathy. This moment in time begs for sacrificial love, the pursuit of the absolute truth of God, and the changed hearts of believers. We have pushed God away as a society and put self first, bringing out many of the worst parts of our being. We were designed by God to love, care, and nurture. Today is the day to push the sin of the world aside and rest in the peace of obedience to God. Not tomorrow. Today.

So TODAY be an encouragement. Be sure you are part of the solution rather than part of the problem. TODAY soften your heart to receive and put into action your faith in our loving God. Acts of kindness and love have power. TODAY live in the light of Christ, being transparent in your love and obedience to God. We need to be bold in our faith and unafraid of sin. God has already won the eternal battle for us. TODAY live a refreshed life, sure and comforted by the promises of God. He will never fail us and will never leave us. In and through Him we can live as saved souls, free to love freely. TODAY be an encouragement and example. TODAY live free. TODAY rest in Him. TODAY.

We all need to feel love and be comforted. That love is in Christ. We all need to feel meaningful. You mean everything to Christ. We all need to find peaceful rest. Christ is the source of that contentment. We all need to feel part of something bigger than ourselves. Understand that we serve a magnificent, powerful God. No matter what our past is, we can live forgiven. No matter what happens tomorrow, we can hold firm to the knowledge of the love of Christ. In the present, live TODAY with the knowledge that you are loved. Be encouraged and be an encouragement. Live with a soft heart, knowing that Christ is served through your love toward others. TODAY belong to Him.

"So that your trust may be in God,
Today I propose to make your way known to you."

PROVERBS 22:19

EARTHENWARE JARS

"We are only the earthenware jars that hold this treasure,
to make it clear that such an overwhelming power
comes from God and not from us."

2 CORINTHIANS 4:7

The value of a treasure is not in the packaging, it is what is on the inside that counts. You can put a diamond in a pretty box or a paper sack. It is still a diamond. Over and over again, God chose to use people throughout the Bible who were not the most popular or most glamorous. He used real people, with all their faults and sordid histories. People filled with flaws, impurities, and shortcomings were used as vessels for the divine purposes of God. The package may not have been pretty, but the treasure inside was divine.

God can and does use every believer, entrusting His Holy Spirit inside of them to do the work He has in mind and for His purposes. Despite our impurities, through faith He lives within us. Despite our limitations, through faith we become instruments of God. Despite our human nature, through faith we can be used for heavenly outcomes. Because of His love for each of us, He trusts us. He uses us. He enables us. It is an amazing God that uses real people, in real circumstances, expecting real results. He has chosen to use us as the holder of the ultimate treasure, a relationship with the Almighty God.

By using imperfect people, He allows a perfect message to resonate and His abundant love to be on display. He loves us completely, cracks and all.

When we are at our most vulnerable, the treasure inside of us can bring peace. When we know our imperfections are on display, the power of God keeps us together. When we feel rigid and intolerant, the love of God inside of us can show us the way to understanding and wisdom. The principle aim for believers is to let God find residence inside of them, depending on the treasure and not the package. Letting God dwell in our hearts overshadows the personal flaws we often blame for our situations. He is the overwhelming power that has chosen us, individually, to carry His treasure to the world. He sees us exactly as we are, knows our faults and problems, and has chosen to have a personal relationship with us. His love overpowers the limits we set on ourselves, allowing His Spirit to fill us abundantly.

We may feel like an unworthy vessel, but we are the vessel chosen by God. We are important to Him, loved by Him, and cherished by Him. Apart from Him we are an empty package judged by our exterior. With Him we are the carrier of the Good News of the power, grace, and majesty of God. It is time we see beyond our exterior and see the God that lives inside. He binds the cracks, fixes the broken, and loves the lost. Let His power, the real treasure we hold, be seen in all we do.

"The name of God is a strong tower;
The virtuous man runs to it and is secure."

PROVERBS 18:10

JESUS INTERRUPTED

"So as He stepped ashore He saw a large crowd; and He took pity on them and healed their sick."

MATTHEW 14:14

The plans of Jesus got interrupted. He had just found out His cousin John had been beheaded and Jesus had gone to be alone to grieve. He wanted the peace and quiet of solitude following such terrible news. His time of solitude was quickly interrupted. The moment He steps ashore, He is greeted by a large number of people all thirsting for healing and the attention of Jesus. How would you react? How did Jesus react? At a time of deep sorrow, He reached out. At a time that would be easy to feel self-pity, He felt compassion for all those who gathered. At a time when He had emotional needs, He met the needs of others. An interrupted Jesus reacted in love.

When was the last time you thought of an interruption as an opportunity from God? Jesus looked beyond His present circumstance and not only showed pity, but healed. He turned an interruption into a blessing. He healed His situation with healing. He let love overpower sadness. He poured Himself out for others, not letting the circumstance limit His compassion.

When things are not going according to your plan, do you look inward or outward? Is it possible to accept that interruptions may be a blessing and an opportunity? Can you see, even in difficult times, the needs of others and do something about it? Jesus is our example!

The crowd Jesus faced on the shore left their village on foot to go see Him. They went miles to come into contact with the One who could do miracles. They came broken and in need. They came in wonder. They were not disappointed. Jesus saw their need and healed them. When was the last time you saw someone's need and met it? Are you too busy? Is it not on your timetable? Do you think you don't have enough? Jesus made time. Jesus was interrupted and acted. Jesus poured out Himself in abundance.

Jesus did not have a schedule for every minute or a rehearsed speech to give. He did not live making future plans or putting restraints on His time. He lived in the present moment, willing to be interrupted to see and meet the needs of others. He did not need to plan for His future because it was assured. You have that same assurance leaving you free to live in the moment. Jesus showed us the way to live…full of compassion and action…all to the glory of God. Leave room for God to turn every interruption into a blessing.

"A man's heart plans out his way
But it is God who makes his steps secure."

PROVERBS 16:9

LIVE THE LIFE

"We can be sure that we are in God only when the one who claims to be living in Him is living the same kind of life as Christ lived."

1 JOHN 2:6

The way you live your life is the revelation of what is in your heart. If you identify yourself as a Christian it will be evident by the manner in which you live. You will display the traits that Christ displayed in situations that challenge you. You will have patience, kindness, and love revealed through your life. Humbleness, nobility, and servanthood will be part of your character. Your life will show a godly purpose instead of being subject to the influences of the world.

Will there be times that you fail? Of course. But through your repentance, you will reveal your commitment to Christ. You cannot think, learn, or intend your way to being a Christian. You have to live it! Our actions show ourselves and others what kinds of loyalties, commitments, and priorities we have. We don't want to live a godly life, we want to live a life in God. We want a close, personal, and intimate relationship with God that directs our actions in our daily lives as close to the model of Christ's life as possible.

The world is constantly pulling us away from God with all its temptations and cries for separation from God. Somehow we are supposed to believe in

God, yet base our decisions devoid of His presence. How can we be in God and yet separate ourselves from Him as this secular world demands? You cannot!

We can best show our commitment and obedience to God by the way we consistently live in Him. We cannot pick and choose when to live Christian lives and be in God. We cannot manipulate circumstances with half-truths and be in God. We cannot rationalize our lack of commitment and be in God. Our actions reveal our heart. Our commitments are revealed through our actions. The level of relationship with God is revealed in our attitudes and the manner in which we live out our life. Don't strive to be godly, but let your actions show that you are in God.

"Even at play a child reveals
whether his actions will be pure and right."

PROVERBS 20:11

OBSTACLES

"He said to His disciples, 'Obstacles are sure to come, but alas for the one who provides them!'"

LUKE 17:1

Have you ever been an obstacle? Have you found yourself being part of the problem rather than part of the solution? It has happened to all of us, and it is such an easy trap into which we all fall. It happens when we put ourselves and our ideas ahead of God and His nature. We insist on following man-made customs and rituals, thereby displaying a sense of spiritual superiority which can so easily get in the way of others coming to faith. The world presents enough obstacles as we move to dependence on God and too often "religion" adds to these hardships.

Faith is about a relationship with God. Anything that interferes with nurturing that relationship is detrimental. Instead of impeding, we must be enabling. As a believer, one of our greatest joys is to help others come to faith in Christ.

Be sure you make this path to faith as easy as you can. Think about your own relationship with God. Are you putting your own obstacles in the way of your commitment? What is really important? Everything that we do should be done as if it had eternal consequences, because it does. What is stopping or hindering you from a complete commitment to God and a life of His peace?

Don't make it any harder than the world makes it, but instead actively omit and distance yourself from the things that get in the way of an intimate relationship with God. See if your priorities match the priorities necessary to move closer to Him. Don't just identify the roadblocks you find, remove them.

Pray for the energy, wisdom, and willingness to keep your path headed directly toward God, to keep your relationship with God growing, and to be sure that you are never an obstacle to anyone's spiritual life. The life of a Christian is one that nourishes and encourages, enables and empowers, provides and sacrifices, reveals and assists. Keep your path straight.

"He who lives an honest life will be safe,
He who wavers between ways falls down in one of them."

PROVERBS 28:18

ONE SINGLE SACRIFICE

"He, on the other hand, has offered one single sacrifice for sins, and then taken His place forever, at the right hand of God."

HEBREWS 10:12

One single atonement. One single act of obedience. One single act of love. In one single sacrifice, Christ did it all. The victory was His and we enjoy the fruits of His sacrifice through faith in Him. How blessed are we!

If it weren't for Christ we would be caught in a revolving door of trying to cover the multitude of our sins time and time again. We would never be able to be in full relationship with God. There would always be a sin left uncovered and a nature left unpaid for. Perpetual sacrifice by us could never be capable of taking away our sin. Only the sacrifice of Christ is sufficient to atone, justify, and reconcile us to our heavenly Father. In His one single sacrifice, He changed everything for eternity. He destroyed the barriers between us and Him. He made us able and worthy for intimacy with Him. He paid the price for the sins of the world. How blessed we are!

The power and love that was required by Christ makes Him worthy of our full response. Why should He save me? Because He loves. Why would He suffer for my sake? Because He loves. What can I do to repay Him? You should love as He loves you. Sacrificial rituals cannot take the place of living a life of commitment to love. We try and try to make ourselves right with God, but He has done that work for us. His requirement is faith. His gift is life. Believing in His sacrifice lets us live free to not just know of God, but to know God. The character of God is love and His single sacrifice is proof. We need to look no further than Christ, no deeper than Christ, and no other place than Christ. He has done it all in a single sacrifice. How blessed we are!

There is no need for us to ever feel unworthy when through faith we can be beneficiaries of the work of Christ. How could He possibly love a sinner like me? He is love. It may not make sense to us, but that is what faith is all about. By trusting in His one single sacrifice, we are His children, heirs with Christ to eternity. By living as a saved person through his one single sacrifice we reveal a glimpse of His power and majesty. By loving through the example of Christ's single sacrifice, we can live freely in obedience to His purpose. One sacrifice—a world changed-forever. How blessed we are!

"The wicked do not know what justice means,
Those who fear God understand everything."

PROVERBS 28:5

PSALM 105

Verses 1-5

"Alleluia!
Give thanks to God, call His name aloud,
Proclaim His deeds to the peoples!
Sing to Him, play to Him, tell over all His marvels!
Glory in His holy name, let the hearts that see God rejoice!
Seek God and His strength,
Seek His face untiringly;
Remember the marvels He has done,
His wonders, the judgments from His mouth."

MY PERSPECTIVES

THE TRUE LIGHT

"This is the message we have heard from Him and declare to you: God is light; in Him there is no darkness at all."

1 JOHN 1:5

Are you hiding anything from God? There is nowhere to hide in pure light. Everything is seen, everything is revealed. How wonderful it is to know that God is light. He is not hiding anything from us. There are no surprises ahead that would make us mistrust God. His light reveals the sin in us and overpowers the darkness of that sin. How can there be darkness in the midst of pure light? How can there be the darkness of sin when it is overpowered by brightness? You cannot be in the light and in the shadows at the same time.

The revelation of His light is the reason we must strive to walk as closely to God as we can, allowing His light to destroy the natural darkness in our lives. "In Him there is no darkness at all." Pure light, pure forgiveness. Light illuminates, reveals, and has power and dominance over darkness. Let us pray that we stay close to the source and cherish the Holy light of Jesus Christ.

Do you have any darkness today? You can't hide it from God. Allow His pure light to destroy that darkness. Bring the shadows out into the open to be washed away by the light.

This passage assures us that God is pure. Light penetrates all shades of darkness. It destroys the darkest black to the lightest shades of gray. No sins are able to hide from the power of pure light. Be assured that whatever your sins are, they can be washed away like the darkness by the light of truth of Jesus Christ. Live your life today as someone walking in light. You are a forgiven being blessed by grace. Stay close to the source, Jesus Christ.

"The light of virtuous men burns bright,
the lamp of the wicked goes out."

PROVERBS 13:9

WHILE WE HAVE THE CHANCE

"While we have the chance, we must do good to all, and especially to our brothers in the faith."

GALATIANS 6:10

The time is now! There is no reason to wait. This verse is a call to action that requires a consistent commitment to always doing what is right. Whatever is in front of us, we need to have an attitude of being part of the best outcome and approaching everything with love. We are called to do good.

In every situation we have a choice. Will we be part of a God-focused solution, or will we be part of the problem? Will we build up or tear down? Will we put the truth first, or will we compromise and water down our beliefs? Will we build relationships, or will we put up roadblocks that keep people apart? Accept the challenge to see whatever is before you through the lens of Christ. We are called to do good; we are called to love.

Sometimes we become paralyzed in our lives because the problems seem too big for us to solve. Our mission is to solve one problem at a time, to love fearlessly and fully, and to approach every challenge with the heart of a servant of Christ. We cannot let chances pass us by, expecting others to meet the challenges that we see. Every day is our chance to do what is good. Every day is our chance to show the love of Christ to others. Every day is our chance to let Christ work through us to meet the needs of others. The time is now. We must do good to all.

We need to not only do what is right, but also support others who endeavor to do the same thing. Doing good is not easy. In fact, it is often the hardest thing to do. If we do not approach life with faith the right thing is not the natural thing to do. With faith, we are empowered to live free and do good with joy, energy, and confidence. The good thing is always God's way. The good thing is always the right way. The good thing is our response to the love of God. Let the good thing be your guide.

One act of kindness at a time can change attitudes, outcomes, and lives. We do what is good knowing that we act with the power of God on our side. We do what is good without motive and without condition. We do what is good because our faith tells us it is the right thing to do.

Do not let any chances slip by you. Grab on to the opportunities to witness and love for Christ. There is eternal value in every effort to do good for Christ. Get busy.

"Do not refuse a kindness to anyone who begs it,
If it is in your power to perform it."

PROVERBS 3:27

OTHERS FIRST

"Always consider the other person to be better than yourself, so that nobody thinks of his own interests first but everybody thinks of other people's interests instead."

PHILIPPIANS 2:4

How different would this world be if we all followed this instruction? Today's world tries desperately to go in the opposite direction. We are told time after time to demand our own rights and look out for ourselves. We are told no one will help us so it is up to us to put ourselves first, no matter who might get in the way. Being humble is looked upon as a weakness, as a character fault, or as something to apologize for. We constantly notice the shortcomings of others, often in a vain attempt to rationalize to ourselves our superiority.

How is it possible to be of one mind when everyone is putting himself or herself first? This is why the ways of the world are failing and why we need to listen and obey the words of this verse. Over and over again we are told in the Scriptures to be humble, not presuming ourselves any better than anyone else. We are all blessed with the same promises from God and have been given different gifts, all of which have value to God. Being humble is basic to the character of a Christian. It is not our place to be served, but to serve.

Anything that is detrimental to others in the long run is detrimental to us. We are to be good stewards of the gifts that God has given us in His wisdom and not let our attitudes in any way divide ourselves.

How can you help someone today? Will your attitude be one of service? Can you see the good in all of God's creatures and allow God to be the judge? Place yourself with your attitude in a position to use the gifts that God has given you in a positive way, yearning to bring others closer to God. Be the best steward of God's gifts that you can be. Never let your attitude of your own importance get in the way of other's faith. Be prepared to be a servant to others. Let God use your humility and willingness to elevate others to further His kingdom. Stay humble.

"The arrogant heart is abhorrent to God,
be sure it will not go unpunished."

PROVERBS 16:5

YOU ARE RESCUED

"...who in order to rescue us from this present wicked world sacrificed Himself for our sins..."

GALATIANS 1:4

Are you feeling overwhelmed with your circumstances? You have been rescued. Are you unable to break away from sin? You have been rescued. Are you having trouble finding any answers to your problems? You have been rescued. Is there no satisfaction in what the world has to offer? You have been rescued.

Through Christ's selfless, sacrificial act of His crucifixion and His victory over death, we have all been rescued. His sacrifice covers it all, once and for all. On our own, we are in a no-win position, destined for failure at every turn. The world will chew us up with no mercy. Wickedness is everywhere and is not going away until the last day.

The good news is that God knows our sinful nature and has provided the only way out: faith in the blood of Christ. There is no solution that we can possibly come up with on our own. Salvation comes only through Christ and His sacrifice. What a loving God we have!

Notice this verse says He sacrificed Himself for OUR sins. His sacrifice is personal. He knows you, your past sins and your future sins. He was willing to pay the price for YOU. Despite our own wickedness, He chose to rescue us, not because of what we do, but because of who we are, a child of God. He rescues US, personally and completely. This short verse embodies the entire Gospel. What a loving God we have who personally cares for each of us so much.

There is no reason to live in fear. There is no need to live in anxiety. The assurance and knowledge of God's plan is all we need. You have already been rescued. Live in that joy.

"No harm can come to the virtuous man,
But the wicked have their fill of troubles."

PROVERBS 12:21

IS IT WORTH IT?

"The love of money is the root of all evils and there are some who, pursuing it, have wandered away from the faith, and so given their souls any number of fatal wounds."

1 TIMOTHY 6:10

Money. We need it. We want it. We sacrifice for it. We pursue it at all costs. Is all that effort worth it?

God. We need Him. He wants us. He sacrificed for us. The cost of our sin is paid. Are we worth it?

We live in a world that revolves around the pursuit of more: More money, more stuff, just more. We tell ourselves that if we just had a little more of what we can buy, we would find happiness. We are wrong. A heart set on money is never satisfied. How much do we need? The honest answer for most of us is we think we need just a little more than we have. We always reach for more and continually come up empty. When money becomes our god, we have set ourselves up for a life of frustration. When we wander away from faith, we have set ourselves up to miss out on the hope and peace found only in Jesus. Stay on the path that satisfies. That path will lead us to Jesus.

We have many choices that confront us daily. What do we pursue? Are we willing to love God so much that money loses its allure? Can we find contentment in a promised eternal life? Can we be satisfied with a life and attitude focused on giving more than taking? Can we rest in the hope of Jesus, letting our worth be found in following Him instead of pursuing money? Is being a follower of Jesus worth more than being a pursuer of stuff? These choices have eternal ramifications. These choices reveal where our real heart and soul are, either with Jesus or on things. Following the money trail wherever it goes, can be fatal to our souls.

We can do a lot of good in this world with our money, as long as we approach it as a steward of a gift from God. The love of money must never replace our love of God. Anything that we put before God will never bring the satisfaction that we can find through faith. Instead of "following the money" to see the ambitions that enslave us, we should "follow the trust" that makes us a child of God. Instead of building a portfolio, we must build on the love we have been shown by God. Instead of growing our assets, we need to be adding to our faith.

Contentment is a hard thing to realize and make part of our character. It seems like the demand for more never ends, and the pressure builds and builds, increasing the temptations for shortcuts and to take advantage of others. There is no competition for the love of Jesus. There is no entry-level position to start earning the love of God. There are no pre-qualifications to make us worthy of His love. Never let money get in the way or lead you away from the grace of God. We are worth His investment when we put the love of God above everything else. God never fails. Pursue Him with all your might.

"What good is money in a foolish hand?
To purchase wisdom, when he has no sense?"

PROVERBS 17:16

ONLY ONE THING IS NEEDED

"But the Lord answered: 'Martha, Martha,'
He said 'you worry and fret about so many things,
and yet few are needed, indeed only one.
It is Mary who has chosen the better part;
it is not to be taken from her.'"

LUKE 10:41-42

What is really important? These verses make it unmistakably clear that only one thing is truly important. In this story of the two sisters, it is Mary who has chosen the better priority. She placed herself at the feet of Jesus and listened to Him speaking. What could be more important than that? Not only did she place herself with Him, but she also listened to Him.

Is that how you spend your time? Does your life reveal the importance of being in close proximity with Jesus, at His feet, eager to listen? Nothing else comes close to the importance of a close, personal relationship with Jesus.

Martha, on the other hand, was busy worrying and fretting. She was busy doing a good thing, preparing and serving a meal for Jesus. However, she had missed the point. We can have good intentions and work very hard at what we think is important, but still miss out on the relationship. Like so many of us, she was caught up in the details. She was agitated because she felt she was doing all the work while her sister was with Jesus. She even asked the Lord to tell her sister to get busy and help.

But Jesus' answer was very direct and clear. We need to only identify with one thing, our relationship with Jesus. Listening to the Word of God must be the primary driving force in our everyday lives.

Both parts of Mary's actions were important. First, she made herself available to Jesus. He was her priority. Nothing else really mattered. She would not be distracted. Second, she listened to Him. There was a real interaction between Jesus and Mary. The opportunity to learn and grow would not pass her by. Mary's heart was in the right place.

We can easily be distracted by all the things that go on around us. We spend so much time and effort worrying about things that are really not important to what Jesus has in mind for us. Which priority will you choose? Will you find yourself at Jesus' feet listening, or will you be distracted by things that don't matter? Find yourself at Jesus' feet and listen.

"A man's conduct may strike him as upright,
God, however, weighs the heart."

PROVERBS 21:2

PSALM 34

Verses 7-10

"The angel of God pitches camp
Round those who fear Him;
And He keeps them safe.
How good God is—only taste and see!
Happy the man who takes shelter in Him.
Fear God, you His holy ones:
Those who fear Him want for nothing.
The young lion may go empty and hungry,
But those who seek God lack nothing good."

MY PERSPECTIVES

STAND FIRM

"Because of the increase in wickedness, the love of most will grow cold, but he who stands firm to the end will be saved."

MATTHEW 24:12-13

Wickedness continues to grow, becoming so pervasive that we are desensitized by it. It has the ability to steal the passion of our love. With the world condoning more and more sin, the lines between right and wrong become more and more fuzzy, blurring to the point where no line exists at all. The fight for right seems insurmountable in a world of wickedness. It all sounds so hopeless and bleak.

How can we survive in these circumstances? Praise God for His promises! We are promised salvation! No matter what conditions surround you, do not give in. Stand firm to the end, and we are promised to be saved. Our job is to trust in the Lord and to simply do what is right. We are to not allow our love to grow cold, but instead to let our love burn brightly. We cannot focus on the wickedness of the world and we cannot let that wickedness take the heat of our passion for the Lord away from us. It is so easy to grow cold and desensitized, degree by degree, decision by decision, day by day. Stand firm! Do what is right, decision by decision, moment by moment, day by day.

Let your love for the Lord be the reason behind your actions, not the reasoning of the world. So often we try to take the easy way out, compromising our beliefs. The world almost forces us into rationalizing behavior which we know does not reflect the love of God. Stand firm in your daily walk with God. Keep yourself centered in God through continual prayer. Thank God for His promises and trust Him.

Ask yourself today if your love is growing colder. How firm are you standing for the Lord? The promises of God stand before us. Stand firm to the end and you will be saved!

"Folly appeals to a man with no sense,
the man of discernment goes straight forward."

PROVERBS 15:21

A LIFE OF LOVE

"To love is to live according to His commandments:
This is the commandment which you have heard since the beginning,
to live a life of love."

2 JOHN 6

The message is not new, but it is very direct. Living a life of love is not an emotion; it is a commitment to action. It is your dedication to a purpose and a willingness to embrace a discipline that puts concern for others above concern for yourself. It is a commitment to follow the commandments of God in all circumstances.

The challenge is two-fold. First we must be willing to accept God's command and be willing to rely on doing what is right, without regard to our personal circumstances. Second, we must commit ourselves to living a life of commitment to His command. Can your life be characterized as a life lived according to His commandments in all situations? When faced with everyday decisions, do you make your commitment to His commandments a priority? Is your life one of true love?

This verse very simply reminds us what staying in the will of the Lord is all about—living a life of love, God's love. We have been given the guidelines to live the life of love. Despite how complicated we try to make it, the directions are very simple: live according to His commandments. There is no room for rationalization or "convenient commitment." Living a life of love is continual, consistent, and meaningful. Make yours a life of God's true love.

"Commend what you do to God,
and your plans will find achievement."

PROVERBS 16:3

BE COMPASSIONATE

"Be compassionate as your Father is compassionate."

LUKE 6:36

Webster's definition of compassion: sympathetic consciousness of others' distress, together with a desire to alleviate it

What a great challenge Christ's words set before us. He asks us to mimic in awareness and action the ultimate example we find in the Father of complete compassion. The attribute of compassion is foundational in our understanding of the holiness, purity, and character of God. Compassion is not just something the Father demonstrates. It is who He is. God knows intimately our anxieties and has put forth the ultimate means to bring us true peace. God is love, God is mercy, and God is compassion.

Notice this verse is written in present tense. It does not say to be compassionate because the Father was compassionate. It says be compassionate as your Father IS compassionate. These words are personal, intimate, and life changing. He is YOUR Father. He has shown YOU mercy and compassion. He calls YOU to identify directly with Him as He is glorified by the way YOU show compassion. How can you witness your belief every day? Be compassionate.

True compassion means that we have to look beyond ourselves and see the distress others are facing. We face a world that is screaming at us to put ourselves first, telling us we deserve everything and we deserve it now. Christ is telling us to put ourselves aside and not only realize the plight of others, but do something about it. We are called to de-escalate strife and be peacemakers. We are called to forgive even when it does not seem fair. We are called to keep our judgments to ourselves and treat everyone equally. We are called to be willing to sacrifice for the good of others. We are called to be compassionate.

Christ in this verse is asking us to take on His character. He does not say act with compassion, instead He says BE compassionate. Compassion needs to be part of our character that shows itself on a continual basis. Just as compassion is part of the character of God, so too should compassion be part ourselves. Compassion is an active attribute, calling on our empathy and mercy to be on display to honor the Father. Compassion shows to whom we belong. Be a child of God.

The world we live in needs compassion. Opportunities to reveal the love of God to those around us are never far away. Showing the compassion of the Father to others is both a gift and a responsibility to each of us. Let your compassion shine!

"Do not refuse a kindness to anyone who begs it,
If it is in your power to perform it.
Do not say to your neighbor. 'Go away! Come another time!
I will give it you tomorrow', if you can do it now."

PROVERBS 3:27-28

OUR CONSTANT CREATOR

"So even those whom God allows to suffer must trust themselves to the constancy of the creator and go on doing good."

1 PETER 4:19

The world around us seems to be changing faster and faster. It is hard to keep up as technology creeps into our lives more and more each day. We are bombarded by differing opinions. It is difficult to know what to believe. We struggle wondering what we can depend upon and what we can hold as absolute truth. Throughout it all, there is only one person that remains constant. God. He is the same yesterday, today, and tomorrow. Constancy is part of His character. It is His essence. His promises never change. His grace never ends. His love has no bounds.

He is dependable and trustworthy, always full of grace and true love. It is because of this constancy that we can have the full, dedicated hope found only in Him. He will never let us down, leave us out in the cold, or take away His promises. We may suffer, but we are never away from His grace. We may feel overwhelmed, but His strength and power will always see us through. We may feel beaten down, but He will never leave us broken. As we mature in Christ and understand the depth of His love, we can rest assured that He has us in His hands and will never leave us. He knows our sufferings, our limits, and our abilities. He provides healing, comfort, and possibilities. It is in our weakness that we recognize His strength the most. In our suffering we call on Him and can find comfort. The peace of the creator is a peace that will see us through every circumstance and every heartache. The love of God never changes.

One of our greatest challenges in life is to continue to focus on doing good in every circumstance. We see things change in our lives, and we react with selfish motives. We live with a survival of the fittest attitude instead of survival through faith. Because God is constant we can trust, honor, and rely on Him. We can go on doing good because we have faith in a faithful God. We can love for no reason at all, other than the knowledge that we are loved by the Creator. We can find peace in the midst of turmoil, rest in the midst of chaos, and comfort in the midst of pain. We continue to go on doing good because the best part of us is the Holy Spirit within us, encouraging and empowering us to serve, honor, and help. We continue to go on doing good because the power of the love that God has for each of us overpowers our guilt, fear, and apprehensions. We find rest and peace in every situation because we KNOW we are loved, we KNOW we are heirs in Christ, and we KNOW our eternity is secure. We can trust in these facts because of the constancy of God and the constancy of His love.

It is not the way of the world, but a Christian can be thankful even in the midst of a trial. A Christian can place trust in Him, especially when we see how little power we have over our circumstances. A Christian can find peace when we rely on His grace to calm our hearts. Everything changes, but not God. Relative truth changes, but not the absolute truth of God.

"He stands guard over the paths of justice,
He keeps watch on the way of His devoted ones."

PROVERBS 2:8

THE STRUGGLE

"I cannot understand my own behavior. I fail to carry out the things I want to do, and I find myself doing the very things I hate."

ROMANS 7:15-16

How do we want to see ourselves as believers? Are we devoted, committed, and bold? Are we slaves to Christ?

What is the reality of our natural condition? Are we selfish, self-absorbed, and weak? Are we slaves to the world?

These verses tell us without any question that, if left to ourselves, living under our own power, we are destined to a life of frustration. What it shows us is that the material, physical part of our being is at odds with our spiritual relationship with Christ. We are not perfect! Paul was not perfect! To expect to be able to be perfect in our carnal state is an exercise that can only lead to guilt and conflict. We cannot earn our way into a relationship with God!

Paul's message and example tells us that our salvation will come with life in the Spirit, not in the world. We may struggle inwardly, but God is bigger, stronger, and in command of the larger picture. He loves us DESPITE our struggle, DESPITE our failures, and DESPITE our sins. He loves us where we are and for who we are, children of the most-high God.

Paul's example was one of working constantly toward the realization that Christ and only Christ allows us to have a relationship with God. Our goal is a life with the Spirit as a foundation toward faith, through the grace of God, not of ourselves. Paul is telling us despite the fact that we all fail, God never does. These verses appear directly after Paul has described the function of the Law as it reveals our inability to be perfect. Because of the Law, we are aware that we will always fall short and we must rely on Christ, not ourselves, to be justified and restored to a relationship with God.

Paul was frustrated. He knew how important depending on the Spirit was and how important it was to change our behavior to be as Christ-like as possible. How many times have we all been frustrated by our actions? How many behaviors do we all struggle with that we know fall short of the Spirit-filled life? Are you frustrated by this struggle like Paul?

Paul may have been frustrated, but he never took his eye off of Christ. We may struggle, but with Christ on our side, we will never be defeated. To struggle is part of the life we will live here on earth. The good news is we have both the promise and the guarantee of the grace of God. And despite our behavior, a life dedicated to the Spirit sets us free to be a true child of God.

God knows we are not perfect, but loves us anyway. God knows we struggle and offers His comfort. Even when we cannot understand ourselves, God knows. Take comfort and find peace in Him.

"The name of God is a strong tower,
The virtuous man runs to it and is secure."

PROVERBS 18:10

A SHINING LIGHT

"In the same way your light must shine in the sight of men,
so that, seeing your good works, they may give the praise
to your Father in heaven."

MATTHEW 5:16

Every action we take reveals our character and commitment to God. Every action speaks to the reverence and holiness of our heavenly Father. As a child of God our actions are a representation of our faith and the depth of relationship we have with Him. Our actions reveal the trust we have in God.

What does your life reveal? Is your light, the power and trust in God within you, shining brightly? Is your light shining so brightly that those around you see the power of God in action? Our light brings compassion, empathy, and love to a world in desperate need. Our light brings attention and importance to the character and presence of our living, caring God. Our light reflects the love that God has for each of us. Our light makes us different from the world. That difference should be obvious, real, and transparent. Our light should serve to draw others to God because of our commitment and reliance on Him.

Our actions emanate from our motivation to serve Him and bring His glory to every situation. Obedience and sacrifice are expected, not excuses.

Humility is a virtue, not a sign of weakness. Christians stand out and shine when challenged and know that their faith and trust in God, not self-reliance, are the sources of true peace in all circumstances.

Your peace and confidence should make others wonder what makes you so different from the world and seek a relationship with God. Your motivation for good works will make others notice the kindness of your spirit. Your gentleness and compassion will make others aware that your motivations are pure.

What is your secret? The secret is a loving Father in heaven. The secret of faith and trust are the sacrificial acts that Christ has provided for us to radiate to the world. The secret of peace that can only come from God is ours to display at every opportunity. The secret that is ours as Christians is grace.

We have a great responsibility to shine for God. Our actions must be pure, honest, and true. Our light is a constant witness to God's love. Be that light that the world so desperately needs. Reflect Him at all times. Don't keep it a secret!

"Let God be pleased with a man's way of life,
And he makes his very enemies into friends."

PROVERBS 16:7

PSALM 8

Verses 3-6

"I look up at Your heavens, made by Your fingers,
At the moon and stars You set in place-
Ah, what is man that You should spare a thought for him,
The Son of Man that You should care for him?
Yet You have made him little less than a god,
You have crowned him with glory and splendor,
Made him lord over the work of Your hands,
Set all things under his feet."

MY PERSPECTIVES

TRANSPARENT

"But if we live our lives in the light, as He is in the light, we are in union with one another, and the blood of Jesus, His Son, purifies us from all sin."

1 JOHN 1:7

Transparent. Out in the open. Open to criticism. Harmonious with others. No secrets. Identified with Christ. Do these descriptions fit you? Living life in the full light can be difficult, but it comes with a promise. The blood of Christ lets us get out of the shadows, away from the darkness, and into the full freedom that comes from living in His light. In His light we are purified. In His light we are forgiven. In His light we are without sin. Living in His light we are saved.

Too often we let people see only what we want them to see, holding back because of our guilt and hypocrisy. Too often we try to fool God with the same agenda. Being open leaves us vulnerable, so we hide certain things to avoid pain. Too often we try to hide from God. The light illuminates our inadequacies and shortcomings, so we stay in the shadows. God already knows everything about you and loves you anyway. When we live away from the light, we live alone and are isolated. In the light, we live free and in harmony.

In the light, we can see, understand, and receive the grace of God. We can get a glimpse of the power and glory of God. We can see His power to save us and others as we come together, unified by His blood. We are enlightened to faith. In His light, we are loved and we love.

How we live our lives matters. The manner in which we prioritize and commit our time and effort testifies to what we believe. Living a life open and free speaks to our faith and trust in Jesus. Committing to unity with others in Christ magnifies and glorifies Christ. A transparent life is a trusting life and is something we should all strive for. In the darkness of our sin, we hide, but in the light of the blood of Jesus, we live. Let Him do His miracle in your life as you live in the light.

"The path of the virtuous is like the light of dawn,
Its brightness growing to the fulness of day."

PROVERBS 4:18

GROW SMALL

"He must grow greater, I must grow smaller."

JOHN 3:30

The key to self-awareness for a Christian is realizing that there is something much greater than ourselves: Christ. The highest honor goes to Him. The highest glory goes to Him. The highest praise goes to Him. The words of this verse were spoken by John the Baptist as He was telling His followers how much greater Christ is than himself. John wanted his followers to realize the deity and majesty of Jesus and to tell everyone that Jesus was truly God. John knew his place.

This is a selfish world. We are surrounded by stimuli that uplift service to self over everything else. Humbleness is often seen as weakness; obedience is considered unfair. We are told we deserve what we want, when we want it. We place ourselves first with God being a very distant concern, used only in emergency or out of desperation. John had a much different message.

As we let God grow in our hearts, we grow smaller in our demands. This is strength. Notice this verse says to GROW smaller. Humility and obedience are traits we can grow into as we let God be God. A mature Christian is one that puts God first in all situations. His life is one spent with God, recognizing the enormity of God. It is a life spent honoring God, recognizing God is the source of our entire being. It is a life spent loving God, because God first loved us. It is a life of commitment, built on service and humility. It is a life that happily builds God up at every chance and places God at the center of our entire being.

Smaller does not mean weaker. There is strength in growing God in our lives as we let His power be the driving force of our lives. Smaller does not mean less significant. God values each of our lives and loves always and forever. Smaller does not mean we are alone. God has always had a plan for every life and that life can come to reality as we push ourselves aside and let God reign. In the process of letting God grow larger we are transformed into people that know our place, the beloved children of God.

"A man's heart plans out his way,
But it is God who makes his steps secure."

PROVERBS 16:9

REST

"Then He said to them, 'You must come away to some lonely place all by yourselves and rest for a while; for there were so many coming and going that the apostles had no time even to eat."

MARK 6:31

Rest. We know it is important. We know we need it. But do we make it a priority? One definition of rest is "a means to relax into something and let it support you." When was the last time you relaxed into Jesus and let Him support you? Despite the hustle and bustle of your daily life and all the demands of the world, when was the last time you were alone with Christ? When was the last time you felt the security and comfort of the Lord as you rested in His care? In this verse Jesus was talking to the apostles who had just returned from their missionary work and had been experiencing the pressures of ministry, travel, crowds, and witnessing for Christ. They were spent physically and were in need of refreshment. Jesus did not recommend a short break or a change in the schedule. He said you MUST come away. You MUST rest. You MUST be alone with Jesus.

God designed us to rest. God designed us to be refreshed. God designed us to spend time alone with Him. A worn-out Christian cannot serve Christ to the fullest. We should all be intentional about our rest, yet too often we fill our schedules and calendars to the maximum. We squeeze so much into our lives that time alone with God is pushed aside. Jesus wants to rest with us.

Have you ever felt empty, like you have no more to give? Have you ever felt like the demands of your life push time with Jesus aside? Have you ever felt overwhelmed by the world? Jesus knows we experience these feelings and wants us to value one of His gifts to us…rest. He wants us renewed, refreshed, and invigorated for Him. He wants us committed, focused, and dependent on Him. He wants us rested, secure, and strengthened.

God will support you in your rest. He will renew and refresh you. Time alone with Him will nourish your body and soul. Rest. Accept His peace. Accept His comfort. Let Him support you.

"But whoever listens to me may live secure,
will have quiet, fearing no mischance."

PROVERBS 1:33

ALL PARTS SHARE

"If one part is hurt, all parts are hurt with it.
If one part is given special honor, all parts enjoy it."

1 CORINTHIANS 12:26

People are hurting, and we all feel it. We cannot distance ourselves, discount, or minimize the pain of others with the knowledge that we are all part of the same creation of God. The pain is real and we all suffer. We are quick to look the other way, avoiding the pain that comes with personalizing the discomfort, injustice, and inequality that surrounds us. We fail to see that if anyone suffers, we all suffer in some way. We were all created for mutual benefit, not exclusion. We have to do better.

As the world continues down a path of selfishness and self-importance, we need to step back and realize that it is to our benefit to lift up everyone. We need to correct injustice when we see it. Everyone must be treated with the love of Christ. We have to do everything in our power to find peace and harmony with everyone. We were created so that we can worship God by showing the love of Christ to everyone. We are obligated as believers to treat everyone as siblings in Christ, literal brothers and sisters, all able to receive the salvation available to us through faith in His grace. We are called to a place of unity, not division. We are called to an attitude of equality, not putting our own importance ahead of anyone. We are called to a place of peace, resting in the grace of God.

Lifting someone up has far-reaching rewards. Acts of kindness and love enrich the giver and the recipient. Anything that moves the kingdom of God forward strengthens the entire body of believers. Anything done in the name of Christ glorifies Him and leads to growth, dependence, and trust in Him. We are all part of one body in Christ, and we all depend upon the health of every part to be fully effective. When any part of the body hurts, it has an effect on the body as a whole. When any part of our society hurts, it has a damaging effect on society as a whole. No part is unimportant, and no part can be overlooked. Every part is necessary, and every part has value. Strengthening others fulfills one of our missions as a Christian as we care for the whole of God's creation.

An empathetic heart can feel and recognize the pain of others. A soft heart sees the best in people and does what it can to ease any pain. An open heart sees the need for equality and identifies with the troubles and pain of others. A heart full of the Spirit does one thing better than anything else. It loves always.

"Do not think of yourself as wise,
Fear God and turn your back on evil:
Health-giving, this to your body,
Relief to your bones."

PROVERBS 3:7-8

AT YOUR SERVICE

"Each of you has received a special grace, so like good stewards responsible for all these different graces of God, put yourselves at the service of others."

1 PETER 4:10

All of us are unique individuals with our own strengths and gifts. These qualities do not happen by accident but are given from God. These qualities are given with purpose and for purpose. We are meant to use these qualities for the glory of God, the betterment of all those around us, and to fulfill the plan that God has for each of us. A steward is someone that manages the assets of another and takes responsibility for proper use and value of that asset. The gifts that you possess belong to God. We may be the vehicle He uses, but the best of us belongs to Him. It is up to us to be sure that we honor God by both valuing and using those gifts for His purposes.

It is important that we take the time to analyze ourselves to recognize the blessings of God in each of us. Whatever the gift and whatever the blessing, it must be put into practice to the glory of God. It seems that too often that we do not see our own personal gifts, which we fail to notice and appreciate as we get caught up in the routine of our lives. What you have to offer is exactly what God wanted to give you. Are you using your talents and gifts?

We are creatures meant to serve others. In a world that has a "me first" mentality it is important that we set ourselves apart and lead a life focused on service rather than self. God has already taken care of our eternity, so we are all free to serve happily, gratefully, and abundantly. God equipped each of us to serve in different ways, all for His glory. Whatever you do, wherever you are, SERVE. Love because you are loved by God, serve because you have received His grace, and honor God with an attitude of humbleness and thanksgiving. God has given us the tools to go to work for Him. Push selfishness and self-promotion aside as you take on a servant's heart. Put into practical application the gifts that God has given you as you honor Him in all that you do.

"A gift works like a talisman for him who gives it:
He prospers whichever way he turns."

PROVERBS 17:8

THE MERCY OF GOD

"In other words, the only thing that counts is not what human beings wants or tries to do, but the mercy of God."

ROMANS 9:16

We can have the best intentions, putting forth our best effort, and still fall short of salvation. This verse very specifically tells us that the mercy of God is the only place to put our trust. God's mercy is not dependent upon our earthly attempts or desires for salvation. God's mercy is just that, mercy, given to us by the grace of God despite our earthly shortfalls.

We are limited by human perceptions and cannot see the larger plan that God has for our lives. We see things moment-by-moment and focus on the fallacy that we can depend solely on our own abilities. Our focus becomes what we think we want and how we plan to obtain our goals. Our plans are flawed, and by placing our focus on our own desires, we discount the deity of God. Our place in God's plan is one of acceptance and trust. Realize that God is in control and thankfully accept God's mercy.

Praise Him, accept Him, and live your life dependent and trusting in God's mercy. We are blessed with a God whose mercy exceeds all our understanding. We are incapable of realizing the magnitude of God's mercy. Let God be God! Commit yourself to living your life bathed in the mercy of

God. Praise God for the realization that we can have complete trust in His mercy. Find ways to mirror God's mercy to others. Realize that we cannot think or will our way to salvation. Depend on the promises of God. His mercy is for you. Depend on it.

"Neither wisdom, nor prudence, nor advice,
can stand in God's presence."

PROVERBS 21:30

PSALM 120

Verse 1

"When I am in trouble,
I call to God,
And He answers me."

MY PERSPECTIVES

HEART AND LIPS—THEY GO TOGETHER

"By believing with the heart you are made righteous; by confessing with your lips you are saved."

ROMANS 10:10

This verse is not the game plan for an easy way to heaven. It is an explanation of how we can move ourselves away from the sinful world that surrounds us toward a life centered in Christ. It lets us know that full commitment in body and soul is our goal as we strive to live a sanctified life.

We must believe in our heart. This goes far beyond knowledge and our acknowledgment that something is a fact. Believing in your heart means that your faith in Christ is at your core. This belief becomes our main source of life, providing the blood we need to live in Him. It represents our firm hope and reliance in something not seen. It is the essence of true faith.

Confessing with your lips is not an oral exercise of repeating a confession. It is the means by which the firm belief in our heart is brought to life. It is the visible means by which our belief is displayed. It is our public action that shouts out loud our believing heart. It shows in every way that Christ is our center and faith is our guiding light. It shows commitment.

The heart alone or the tongue alone do not demonstrate full commitment. We can know the truth in our heart, but if we don't demonstrate that truth we fall short of our responsibilities as a Christian. Believing with your heart is foundational, but it is not the end. Confessing with our lips, our outward being, is necessary, but only noise if it doesn't have meaning. Faith is not based on ritual liturgy and mindless recitations. Faith is alive, inside each believer whose heart is full of the Spirit and demonstrated in all we do.

It makes a difference what we believe and it makes a difference how we profess. A Christ-filled life requires both full belief and servitude to that belief—in Christ. God's promises are real and set before us. We can trust that if we fully release ourselves to Him in faith, heart, and actions, a wondrous eternal future with Him awaits.

"My son, if your heart is wise, then my own heart is glad,
and my inmost self rejoices when from your lips come honest words."

PROVERBS 23:15-16

EVEN WORSE

"They know what God's verdict is;
that those who behave like this deserve to die—
and yet they do it; and what is worse,
encourage others to do the same."

ROMANS 1:32

It is one thing to knowingly sin, but it is another thing to be involved in the downfall of others by encouraging their sin and their separation from God. Isn't this a snapshot of what society faces today? What was once abhorred is now commonplace. What was considered blatant sin is now glorified and glamorized. The person who wants to stand for Christ is characterized as out of touch with reality and intellectually inferior. Man has not changed since Paul wrote these words centuries ago, but today sin is big business and front page news.

We have a great responsibility as God's created creatures to behave in a manner that honors Him. We have an even bigger responsibility to encourage others in their walk with Christ and not be a hindrance to that relationship in any way. Too often we see the world crumbling as man gets further and further away from God as they focus on themselves and their desires instead of what God clearly wants.

In the verses that precede this verse, Paul lays out the behaviors that separate us from God. Envy, wrangling, spite, rebellion, arrogance, depravity, greed, rudeness, and enterprising in sin are all listed as conditions man suffers because they have refused to see it is rational to acknowledge God. It is not that man undertakes these practices without knowledge either, but rather purposefully for their own satisfaction. This is what happens when man puts himself first, instead of God.

Every day we see the results of man thinking creation is his, not God's. The world suffers when the desires of man are put ahead of the desires of God. This verse puts each of us in the crosshairs to acknowledge our responsibility as Christians. Are our actions or inactions encouraging others to sin? Have we let our commitment to Christ get so watered down that God has drifted out of the picture? Are Christians misplacing the root of their salvation as they focus on their present condition rather than their eternity?

We are surrounded by encouragement to sin. What was forbidden is now commonplace. What was shocking is now mundane. What was scandalous is now accepted. What was perverted is now part of daily media. It is up to every Christian to be part of a culture that puts God first and is very cautious to never encourage sin. We must be different, pulling our strength from God. We must put God first and not be overpowered by those who would encourage us to sin. We cannot trade the truth of Christ for the lies of the world. It is a tall task, yet nothing is outside the power of God. When we fail, God is there for us. When we fail, Christ has already paid the price for us. When we fail, our sins have been covered by the blood of Christ. Stand firm in faith and let God lead you day by day.

"The conduct of the wicked is abhorrent to God,
But He loves the man who makes virtue his goal."

PROVERBS 15:9

PUT YOUR HEART IN YOUR WORK

"Whatever your work is, put your heart into it as if it were for the Lord, and not for men."

COLOSSIANS 3:23

Wherever you are, whatever you do, in every situation you have the opportunity to serve God. Do you go about your daily tasks in service to the Lord? Do you perform your work happily and to the best of your abilities?

We are all placed in our individual circumstances for a reason. That reason is God's and God's alone. Why complain and wish for different circumstances when we have God's work before us? Throughout each and every day, we are faced with decisions about who and why we really serve. This verse should make us analyze our motives. Who do we serve: God or man? Is our attitude a godly one, or are we a model of grumbling and worldly approaches?

This verse directs us to not just work with our minds and hands, but also with our hearts. It is easy to tell the difference. Can people tell that your heart is in your work? They should be able to! If your work is as if it were for the Lord, it would go beyond the minimum. It would be completed thoroughly, with loving care. It would treat others with compassion and respect and would be based on goodness and not greed. It would be helpful, kind, compassionate, and the best that we can produce. God would be revealed in each and every action. God wants us to present ourselves as godly people no matter what the circumstance. There is no room for unkind words, inconsiderate behavior, or lack of respect. He wants us to care about our attitudes and actions and be sure that others are served. He wants others to see Himself through our actions and attitudes.

Is your heart really in your work? Check your attitude to see if it is how God would like it. Do you work as if it were for the Lord? What great opportunities we have to witness for God every single day. The Lord deserves your best efforts and the commitment of your heart. In all that you do, do it as if it were for the Lord. It is what He expects, and it is what He deserves.

"The man who is idle at work
is blood-brother to the destroyer."

PROVERBS 18:9

WHY WORRY?

"Can any of you, for all his worrying, add a single cubit to his span of life?"

LUKE 12:25

Worry. It puts a stranglehold on our emotions and outlooks. The more we dwell on it, the more power we give it. Worrying chokes our creativity, dominates our thoughts, and diminishes our spirit. An anxious spirit reduces our potential, blinds us from a heart of thankfulness, and takes power from our faith. When we worry, we are not generous and we are not spontaneous. Worry limits every part of us as we look inward instead of outward. So, why do we still worry?

Obviously we all have concerns that need our attention, but it is the dwelling on those concerns that becomes dangerous. We end up trusting only ourselves, misplacing our priorities and efforts. Much of our worry results from not trusting God and not finding contentment with what He has provided. Our desires are threatened, we worry, and we lose out on other experiences. We forget to thank God, we forget to value what He has given us, and we forget the blessings He has lavishly bestowed on us. Worry pushes God away and focuses on things we cannot control. So, why worry?

With God on our side we can be happy with where we are and what we have. We can put worry aside and know that our lives have a godly purpose, a godly direction, and are subject to godly timing. He has provided solutions that last for an eternity. His love for you is not changed by what you have or what you want in this world. If we have an eternal perspective, we can find peace in every situation, through every hardship, and in every trial. His peace, grace, compassion, and love make worrying unnecessary as we find rest in Him and His mercy. The energy we spend worrying about things we cannot change can be better spent in thanksgiving, praise, and honor for the things we do have. And we have the best thing of all already, a gracious God who calls us His own. Unload your worries on Him, and let His blessings be the power that lets you rely not on yourself, but on God, for what you truly need.

"Worry makes a man's heart heavy,
A kindly word makes it glad."

PROVERBS 12:25

BE PART OF THE POWER

"For the kingdom of God is not a matter of talk but of power."

1 CORINTHIANS 4:20

Words by themselves are nothing but words. We can talk about being a Christian and still fall short of the Kingdom of Heaven. How fortunate we are to know that the Kingdom of God is not just empty words, it is alive with power. The Word of God has the power to change lives, to cleanse souls, and to let us be called a child of God. Every day we use words, but our words do not command the power that God does. The Kingdom of God commands respect because of its truth and authority. The Word is truth and its power changes us.

This verse also warns us about using the Word of God. We should all be very careful to not diminish its impact by saying one thing with verbal conviction while displaying actions which show lack of soulful conviction. You cannot use God's Word as a tool to be used for your own purposes. Do not be confused or mistaken. The Word of God and His kingdom are power. It is the power of God that turns the words we hear into conviction in our souls. Listen to the words, then let your soul embrace them and be empowered by God.

How many times have the words of man let you down? How many times have you fallen short of your promises? The Kingdom of God is not just an abstract thought or a story to be told. The Kingdom of God is about power, the power of salvation, resurrection, and forgiveness. These are eternal gifts, not just words.

Do you trust the power of the Kingdom of God, or are you analyzing the words? Does your life reveal the level of your conviction and confidence? The power is ours as a gift through grace. It gives us both confidence and hope. Today pledge yourself to live with power, the power of the Kingdom of God.

"Every word of God is unalloyed,
He is the shield of those who take refuge in Him."

PROVERBS 30:5

THE RACE

"...we too, then, should throw off everything that hinders us, especially the sin that clings so easily, and keep running steadily in the race we have started."

HEBREWS 12:1

What is it that hinders you from running the race for God? What sinful baggage keeps you from reaching God's goals? It is time for all of us to look closely at what it is that hinders our progress toward God!

Too often we aren't even aware of the sin that clings to us. We have become so accustomed to making excuses and accepting sin as part of our lives that we have difficulty even recognizing the sins that hinder us. This verse describes the sin as "the sin that clings so easily." It takes awareness and self-examination to see that kind of sin, and too often we don't make the effort to see our surroundings and true nature of our situation. We become complacent and lose sight of the sin that surrounds us. This sin acts as extra weight, preventing us from proceeding as we should. It wears us down, taking our enthusiasm and commitment. We lose focus and spend our time with eyes focused on the world and our busy schedules rather than eyes focused on God.

What is necessary is clear! Throw off everything that hinders you. There is no shortage of things that we think are important that take away from our race for God.

Our race should be run with confidence, commitment, and energy. We can be confident knowing God's promises are for each of us and are true. God can be trusted. Committing your life to God fills you with more power and peace than you could ever imagine or manufacture on your own. It is a way of life that changes perception and attitudes and is the only path to true peace. Energy is necessary because God calls us to a life of action, not a life of complacency. The race requires effort and determination, not laziness and a lack of discipline. God doesn't promise the race will be easy, which is why it is so important to cast away everything that will hinder you. His victory is yours!

"In every course you take, have this in mind:
He will see that your paths are smooth."

PROVERBS 3:6

PSALM 28

Verses 6-7

"Blessed be God,
For He hears the sound of my petition!
God is my strength, my shield,
My heart puts its trust in Him;
I have been helped, my flesh has bloomed again,
I thank Him with all my heart."

MY PERSPECTIVES

THE SIMPLE ABSOLUTE TRUTH

"I tell you most solemnly, whoever listens to My words, and believes in the one who sent me, has eternal life; without being brought into judgement he has passed from death to life."

JOHN 5:24

This single verse encapsulates the entire, absolute truth of God. His love for each of us and His grace are right in front of us waiting for us to do two simple things: listen and believe. Forgiveness and peace are available to us right this minute if we would just do two simple things: listen and believe. Our struggles with guilt and doubt can disappear in an instant if we would just do two simple things: listen and believe. Our fears and apprehensions can be put aside so that we might live a life free and confident if we would just do two simple things: listen and believe.

Why do we listen? The Word speaks. The Holy Spirit speaks. We must take the time in our busy lives to set aside quality time to do nothing more than listen. Hear the whispers of God and allow Him to direct your thoughts and actions. Be aware of the importance you put on godly matters rather than temporal matters and let His voice be the one that comes first and foremost. Don't let all the noise of anger and division that seems to surround us drown out the clear voice of integrity, honor, and peace found in God. Filter out the negative voices around you and instead focus on the promises of God and His righteousness. Open your heart to let the messages from God fill it with His abundant love. See things through the lens of Christ, not the lens of the world. In a time when so many things seem to be in turmoil, the voice of God continues to speak truth. Will you listen?

Why do we believe? God is real. God is powerful. God is love. One of the struggles so many of us have is that we may know ABOUT God, but we don't know God. We believe when it is convenient or when we need a miracle in our lives, thinking that God will serve us when we ask. This is not belief. Believing in God is striving for a closer and closer personal relationship with Him as He becomes the Lord of your life. It is acknowledging that God is God, and we are not. It is trusting in His grace rather than our own failing abilities. It is trusting in His power to save, His grace to save, and His love to save. Believing in Him becomes not just something we do, but part of our character as we strive to make Him the core of our being. Go all in. Don't hold back. The evidence of His love is all around if we take the time to look. Will you believe it?

The promise of listening and believing is an eternity without fear, regret, or punishment. It is living in eternity NOW, free to enjoy the love and grace of God. He is the only way. He is life. Listen. Believe.

"Listen, my son, and learn to be wise,
And guide your heart in the way...."

PROVERBS 23:19

INVISIBLE THINGS

"...For visible things last only for a time, but the invisible things are eternal."

2 CORINTHIANS 4:18

In the context of eternity, we are here for only an instant. What will you do with the time? Do you believe in eternity? Most of us would say yes, but what do your actions say? Why is it we have such a hard time taking an eternal view of life? Are what we consider daily problems taking so much of our energy and focus that we have lost sight of the importance of eternity? Why do we let circumstances, not faith, control our behavior?

We are so committed to keeping ourselves out of uncomfortable situations that we forget that out of hardship comes awareness, out of the emptiness of self-reliance comes the fullness of the knowledge of God, and out of the failure of pride comes the humbleness of reliance on God. Put the world in its proper perspective. It is temporary. Put your soul in its proper perspective. It is eternal. God wants you for more than your brief stay here on earth. He wants you in His eternity.

The lessons are clear and repetitive throughout His Word. He knows our nature of greed and self-centeredness and knows that we will fail if left to focus only on the here and now. He has also saved us from this plight. He has given us the eternal prize, given freely to an undeserving mankind through His grace. It is the eternal Good News! His warnings are clear not to get caught up in things, but instead hold fast to the promises that remain unseen.

It is faith that will determine your eternity. It is faith that will change the focus of your life here on earth. It is faith that guarantees your eternity, an eternity in a relationship with Him. Does faith make sense to the world? No. Are your goals the same as the world's? No. Is your trust in the visible or invisible? Invisible. What is your priority? Jesus. Are you more concerned about your body or your soul? Soul.

One goal should be foremost in all our lives, a relationship with God. It is faith in Him, Christ's redemptive sacrifice, and the indwelling of the Holy Spirit that assures us of our invisible eternity. Our faith in the unseen moves us from looking for the things of God to God Himself. He is our security. He is our peace. Look beyond your visible, temporary self and trust in the invisible promises of God. Your eternity depends on it.

"He who trust in riches will have his fall,
The virtuous will flourish like the leaves."

PROVERBS 11:28

THE VALUE OF KNOWLEDGE

"... 'We all have knowledge'; yes, that is so, but knowledge gives self-importance—it is love that makes the building grow."

1 CORINTHIANS 8:1

Data comes at us faster and faster. Facts and figures overwhelm us. We are experiencing a faster growth of technology and information than we could have ever imagined. Are we better for it? As people demand "follow the science," it is easy to lose sight of compassion and morality. More knowledge does not necessarily lead to more love and the reliance on numbers does not necessarily lead to wisdom. In our quest for more and more, we sometimes feel less and less. Don't forget God.

Knowledge is not a substitute for relationship and empathy. We are created as caring beings with the capacity to love. We do things that don't make sense, sometimes just because it is still the right thing to do. We love when we do not have to and sacrifice even when it makes no sense. The grace of God and His love is the most important thing in the world. Keep knowledge in its place.

As we gain more knowledge, it is easy to become more self-reliant. When we think we have it all figured out we push God away and depend only on ourselves. Sometimes we may know a lot but understand very little.

We cannot comprehend the mind of God, but we can put into practice what we know of His nature: God is love. We may not be able to fully understand the heart of God, but we can follow His command to love. We may not understand the fullness of reason for His mercy, but we can reflect His grace through loving action. We must never let the knowledge in our head get in the way of the love in our heart.

Pure knowledge is of no value unless it is accompanied with wisdom. The proper use of knowledge is an art, always underpinned by love. We may increase our knowledge, but we are always under the grace of God, and we need to remind ourselves of the source of our knowledge. He is wisdom.

"The fear of God is the beginning of knowledge;
Fools spurn wisdom and discipline."

PROVERBS 1:7

TRUE RICHES

"Warn those who are rich in this world's goods that they are not to look down on other people; and not to set their hopes on money, which is untrustworthy, but on God who, out of His riches, gives us all that we need for our happiness."

1 TIMOTHY 6:17

All that we need for happiness is given to us by a loving God. It seems so simple, yet we spend so much of our time and effort concerned with the untrustworthy. Why do we feel the need to elevate ourselves in the eyes of those around us? Why do we continue to think we need to provide our own means for happiness? Perhaps we have set our hopes on the things of this world rather than on God.

Ours is a culture that exalts the fallacy that more is better and one should do whatever it takes to get ahead. Our culture tells us that the sacrifice of faith and family is worth the end results of more. The only thing we can be sure of is that if we measure ourselves by worldly standards, no matter how much we have, it just isn't quite enough. We want the best of everything, and we are not patient about getting it.

Here God tells us about the true riches, the riches that are given to us and are trustworthy which come directly from God. There is no reason to look down on anyone else. We are all recipients of the most important of riches, His grace and mercy.

Where will you put your trust today? Will you put your hopes in the ways of the world for your happiness, or will you trust God to give you what you need? The answer to this question will have a direct impact on the way you live your life and what priorities you set for yourself. Time after time the world will fail you if you depend on it for happiness. True peace and happiness can come only from God.

Happiness is elusive when we place monetary goals and importance ahead of our reliance on God. Put your faith and hope in the only things that are trustworthy, the gifts from God's great riches. All that you need is given freely to you by God.

"Rich and poor are found together,
God has made them all."

PROVERBS 22:2

YOUR OPPORTUNITY

"Think of your Lord's patience as your opportunity to be saved..."

2 PETER 3:15

Time. How much time is left? How much more patience does God have with us? To so many of us, it seems like we have all the time in the world. We tell ourselves that tomorrow is another day, and what I didn't get done today I will surely have time to do later. We fool ourselves into believing that broken relationships need time to work out, and we will wait for the right opportunity and setting to make amends. We know we have ongoing sinful behavior, but we leave the changing for another day when it isn't so hard. We allow the everyday annoyances and routines to be a wedge between our heavenly Father and ourselves, hoping that someday things will get better.

The sun continues to rise in the morning and we awake from our sleep each day. It seems as though we can put off until later the things that should have been taken care of yesterday. Procrastination turns into complacency, and lack of urgency turns into unimportance.

How many more opportunities do you have? How many more days will God provide for you? How would you live today if you knew that God's patience was going to end at midnight? Would He find you at peace, being a living example of the joy found in the expectation and fulfillment of His promises? Or would He find you unprepared and living with no sense of urgency or commitment?

Time is a gift from God. It gives us the opportunity to prepare to be saved and to do what is necessary to live our lives according to the patterns and commands that God expects. How long will His patience continue? How many more opportunities do you have to truly accept Him as your Lord and Savior and to live your life accordingly? Do you deserve more chances?

No one knows when His patience will end except the Father, but He has told us that His time will come. There is no doubt He has already shown us more patience than we deserve. Yet we continue to squander His gift of time on ourselves instead of Him. The time for change is now. The opportunity to be saved is now. His patience has provided the chance to be saved now. Your eternal future may rest in how you approach your present.

This is no time to hold back or put off what needs to happen today. May we honor His patience with our commitment, obedience, and faith.

"How long do you intend to lie there, idler?

When are you going to rise from your sleep?"

PROVERBS 6:9

QUIT COMPLAINING

"Do everything without complaining or arguing."

PHILIPPIANS 2:14

God's direction may not be easy at times, but it cannot be more plain. We probably have our own opinion of how and when we should carry out the Word of God, and we can very easily find a way to grumble when our ideas and God's don't quite match up. As believers, we are on God's timetable, not our own. We argue about unimportant things in our churches. We complain about things we would like to see changed. We complain about work. We argue with members of our families. Every time we complain or argue we are vainly trying to elevate ourselves to a decision-making position. How distasteful this must be to God.

Every day we are presented with possibilities to witness, glorious possibilities put before us by God at a particular time. How much harm do we do when we complain about the tasks God has put before us? Just do it! Stop the pettiness in your life and quit making excuses. You have enough time when you are doing the will of God. Our argumentative attitudes only serve to drive an unbeliever even further from the grace of God. How important do you think you are? Are you a better judge of situations than God? Are your opinions so valuable that your actions turn evil? Stop for a moment and ask yourself how many times you complained today or how many disagreements and arguments you had. Were you more concerned about your attitudes or the opportunities put before you by God?

Our command in this verse is very plain. Your heart must be clear of complaining and arguing. Your spirit must be one of compassion and humbleness. Your attitude must be one of joyful duty and responsibility. Our God will be glorified by our obedience and enthusiasm. It is up to you to be a Christian with an enabling attitude.

"The lips of just me silence hatted,
he who voices slander is a fool."

PROVERBS 10:18

PSALM 43

Verses 3-5

"Send out Your light and Your truth,
Let these be my guide,
To lead me to Your holy mountain
And to the place where You live.
Then I shall go to the altar of God,
To the God of my joy,
I shall rejoice, I shall praise You on the harp,
God, my God.
Why so downcast, my soul,
Why do you sigh within me?
Put your hope in God: I shall praise Him yet,
My savior, my God."

MY PERSPECTIVES

KEY TO HAPPINESS

"Remember: Anyone who wants to have a happy life and to enjoy prosperity must banish malice from his tongue, deceitful conversation from his lips: he must never yield to evil but must practice good; he must seek peace and pursue it."

1 PETER 3:10-11

The path to a happy life is laid out before you. Peter is repeating the words of Psalm 34 to serve as a road map for Christians. Notice the importance that is placed on the way we speak. We are to banish malice and deceitful conversation from our lips. Are you careful with your words, or do you sometimes speak before thinking? Words can be so hateful when used incorrectly. Be careful with your words, and don't allow them to be used in any derogatory fashion. This will help you keep your thoughts more positive about others.

Don't yield to evil. Instead, be intentional to practice good. Right living is a habit that needs to be practiced consistently. When your mind is on good, you don't give evil the chance to determine your actions. By remaining focused on good, evil is kept at a distance, thereby limiting its power.

Seek peace and pursue it. True peace requires action. Here we are told to be vigilant in our pursuit, actively seeking peace. Be a peacemaker with your words and actions. Both seeking and pursuing are words of action. Do more than just guard your words and conversations. Make sure your words are constructive and positive. Don't just prevail against evil, but use every occasion to practice good. Happiness and enjoyment can be yours, but it requires positive actions. Commit yourself to the practice of good and enjoy the happiness and prosperity that is promised. It will be yours.

"The wise man sees evil coming and avoids it,
the fool is rash and presumptuous."

PROVERBS 14:16

WHICH WAY?

"When they reached the frontier of Mysia they thought to cross it into Bithynia, but as the spirit of Jesus would not allow them, they went through Mysia and came down to Troas."

ACTS 16:7

Paul, Silas, and Timothy were on their way doing the work of the Lord, spreading the Good News of Jesus Christ. Their intentions were pure and honorable. They thought they knew where they were going and they were on a mission. They were committed to a direction, but Jesus had another plan. Thank God Paul and his companions listened and changed their path. They let the spirit of Jesus lead them, and they obeyed. What lessons can the obedience of Paul, Silas, and Timothy teach us today?

1. God's plan is better than our plan.
2. God's timing is better than our timing. It is not just better, it is perfect.
3. We serve God's plan by following Him, not demanding our own way.
4. Even the most pure intentions must be subject to the will of God.
5. God will lead us, if we listen.
6. Great things happen when we are led by the spirit of Jesus and act.

The entire history of evangelism was changed when Paul followed the spirit of Jesus and went to preach to those whom Jesus had chosen, in the order that He had chosen. God's timing is always perfect and the spirit of Jesus was leading Paul in that perfection. The right word was spoken at the right time. The right men preached at the right time. The right audience was present when the Good News would be most effective. In a word, it was all PERFECT. It was Jesus.

So many times we think we have things all figured out. We have our own roadmap, putting our own priorities above all else. We head where we think we should go and stop where we think we should stop. Planning is fine and necessary, but only when we let Jesus lead us. Choosing a pathway is necessary and effective, if we allow for the possibility for Jesus to change our direction. Focusing on what we think is important is admirable, if we recognize that Jesus has the big picture in mind. We need to go in our direction with an open heart and open mind, always aware of the spirit of Jesus. He will use us and direct us in His timing and for His purposes if we listen and obey.

Paul was probably not the easiest man to get along with. Just before these verses, he had gotten into a fight with Barnabas and Mark. They had parted ways after heated discussions. Paul was strong-willed and totally committed to what he was doing. Changing Paul's mind about anything would have been a challenge. But when it counted, at a time when the spirit of Jesus spoke, he listened and obeyed. The decision to follow Jesus instead of demanding his own way changed history for the benefit of the message of salvation. It must have been a humbling experience for Paul, but he nevertheless obeyed with no hesitation. Paul had a plan that was not perfect. Jesus had a plan that was perfect. Paul listened and obeyed.

Every decision we make and every action we take changes our future. We can live life for our purposes, or we can be led by the spirit of Jesus, ready to change course for Him. In our hurry to do things our way we too often close ourselves off to listening to the spirit of Jesus. Make yourself available to the spirit of Jesus. Listen. Obey. Act. His plan and timing will never be wrong.

"In every course you take, have Him in mind:
He will see that your paths are smooth."

PROVERBS 3:6

MY PERSPECTIVES

PLEASING WITH FAITH

"Now it is impossible to please God without faith, since anyone who comes to Him must believe that He exists and rewards those who try to find Him."

HEBREWS 11:6

There are two components that are essential to faith.

First, you must believe that God actually exists. This means you believe in the being and personality of God, the One who cares and knows you as an individual. He is the creator and the judge of all. He desires a relationship with you. In Him, you can place your trust.

Second, you need to believe that there is a reward for those who try to find Him. Those who believe, trust, and seek Him will be rewarded with eternal life. This acknowledgment changes the way that you live your life. Your belief will form the framework that determines your actions in the pursuit of living a godly life.

Faith is an amazing thing. You believe in what cannot be seen. Your life is changed by promises. You trust in what cannot be proven. God has given us the tools for faith. The Word reveals the nature of God and tells us of the promises of God. We have been given a soul that yearns for purpose, meaning, and fulfillment. We have been given a conscience to know right from wrong. We have been given a mind that wants to seek knowledge. In short, we have been created in the image of God and we have the capacity for reliance on faith.

Thank God that we have the tools at hand to please God. Examine yourself to see if you truly believe in the deity of God. Open your heart to the promises of faith. Trust the tools that God has put before you. His promise is clear. God will reward you!

"To be afraid of men is a snare,
he who puts his trust in God is secure."

PROVERBS 29:25

HOW ARE YOU CLOTHED?

"You are God's chosen race, His saints; he loves you, and you should be clothed in sincezre compassion, in kindness and humility, gentleness and patience."

COLOSSIANS 3:12

You are chosen. All those who, through faith, believe that Jesus Christ is their Savior and that He has paid the price for your sin are chosen to receive the gift of eternal life with Him. He chose us while we were still sinners to be the beneficiaries of His grace. He chose us to be heirs with Christ because of the suffering, death, and resurrection He accomplished. He chose us to be set apart as a living being in a sinful world, to be a place where God dwells. You were chosen by the Almighty God to live a life of freedom in Him.

You are loved. He loves us unconditionally, despite our weaknesses and shortcomings. He loves us fully in spite of our indifference and sins. His love is complete and immeasurable. How blessed we are to have a God who loves us consistently and faithfully. We are accustomed to trusting in the things of this world with all its promises that do not hold true. God is different!

In too many instances we feel like we need to earn love, and we fear that the love from others is not permanent or trustworthy. God is different! He loves us with a depth that we can only imagine. He loves us so completely that He was willing to have Christ suffer and pay the price for each of us, allowing us the opportunity to come to Him in response to His love. God does not put conditions on His love. We do not earn it, buy it, or trade for it. His love is real and never changes. The benefits are right in front of us to receive and respond through faith. In a world that struggles to find truth and consistency, God's love is real, dependable, and always there. God is great.

How are you clothed? How do we respond to the kind of love that God showers on us? How do we reflect this kind of compassion that God shows to each of us? What character traits can we develop to best honor the God of Gods and King of Kings. In this verse Paul lays it out for us very plainly. He lists the traits that as chosen and loved children of God we should make part of our lives. Do we put on these traits and surround ourselves with the nature of God every day?

Actively choose to represent God's love in all that you do. Sincere compassion. Kindness and humility. Gentleness and patience. These are the traits that we should cover every part of our bodies so that we honor our loving God. These are behaviors and attitudes that should be the hallmarks of a Christian. Who could show us more compassion than our heavenly Father? Do the same to others. Who could be more kind to us sinners and show the humility to sacrifice Himself for others than Christ? Do the same. Who could be more patient with a sinful human race and continue to show gentle compassion to His children than God? Do the same.

In the many times in our lives when we feel down and depressed, Paul's words to the Colossians should serve as a good reminder that God is always near. You are chosen. You are loved. By committing ourselves in every circumstance to compassion, kindness, humility, gentleness, and patience we have a constant reminder that God is our source, an unending source, of real love.

"The fool comes out with all his angry feelings,
But the wise man subdues and restrains them."

PROVERBS 29:11

PRACTICAL WISDOM

"For me there are no forbidden things, but not everything does good. True, there are no forbidden things, but it is not everything that helps the building to grow."

1 CORINTHIANS 10:23

As the saying goes, "just because you can, doesn't mean that you do." It seems easy sometimes to separate our spiritual life from our everyday life. We compartmentalize our experiences, not letting the wisdom that comes from God dictate what we do or say. We must be wary not to push God away when we need Him the most. The way we live cannot be separated from what we believe! Our faith in God gives us great freedoms, but those freedoms should never be used in a way that might offend others or move them away from God. We must use our faith wisely, always focused on furthering the kingdom of God. With freedom comes responsibility.

The manner in which we live always has a consequence. What we do is either building up or tearing down. Our actions have influence on others and represent what we believe. Our character and how we choose to exercise our freedoms reveal much about whom we believe. Our ability to discern the pathway toward growth and good shows the maturity of our faith. Our commitment to revealing our faith through compassionate love reflects our trust in our compassionate, loving God. Our faith requires us to always build and always grow. With freedom comes responsibility.

Because of His grace we can live with joy and assuredness, having been saved through Christ. It is in that spirit that we are expected to be assets to His Kingdom. We must never be complacent in our faith as we strive to mature and grow in our commitment to God and be wise in our actions. We must use our freedom in every way, every day, to apply our faith with purpose and compassion as a child of God. We must always strive to do the right thing, at the right time, for the right reasons. If we never lose sight of God, we will succeed.

Embrace the responsibility of your freedom and let the wisdom of God keep you growing.

"For God Himself is giver of wisdom,
From His mouth issue knowledge and discernment."

PROVERBS 2:6

NOWHERE TO HIDE

"'How did you get in here, my friend, without a wedding garment?' And the man was silent."

MATTHEW 22:12

The person in this parable had been invited to the eternal wedding feast: the Kingdom of Heaven. He had answered the invitation but was not clothed in the necessary garments. He was not allowed to remain at the wedding.

How are you clothed? What does your appearance say about your faith? Have you wrapped yourself in the righteousness of Christ, or are you wearing the clothing of the world? Have you prepared yourself for a festival of Christ or a tribute to yourself? This verse goes beyond speaking about clothing, but speaks to our representation, testifying to where we place our trust. This person in the story was not prepared. He did not recognize the importance of the wedding or his attitude toward the event.

"And the man was silent." There was nothing he could say. No excuses would do. His lack of preparation was evident. His outward actions did not meet the requirements. He had not put himself in a relationship with the king. There was nowhere to hide. He had wrapped himself up in the wrong clothes. He had not realized the importance of the wedding and He did not honor the king with his ability to clothe himself correctly.

What is your appearance? Does it radiate Christ? Are you clothed in His righteousness? Will you celebrate with the King or expect to stay at the wedding on your own terms? Will you be able to answer with joy and confidence when asked about your preparedness? Will your faith in the King let you celebrate or will your faith in yourself have you removed from the wedding?

Without Christ there is nowhere to hide. With Christ there is nowhere not to celebrate. Without Christ there is no answer. With Christ our lives can shout the love of Christ. Without Christ we know our own self is not enough. With Christ, we live knowing Christ is more than enough.

Put on the clothes of Christ and know you are ready and prepared for the feast. Christ has already answered for you…there is no need to hide when Christ has been revealed and you wear Him proudly. There is no need for anyone who has faith in Christ to be silent.

"When a man has a ready answer he has joy too;
How satisfying is the apt reply."

PROVERBS 15:23

PSALM 139

Verses 1-3

Verses 23-24

"God, You examine me and know me,
You know if I am standing or sitting,
You read my thoughts from far away,
Whether I wall or lie down, You are watching,
You know every detail of my conduct."
"God, examine me and know my heart,
Probe me and know my thoughts;
Make sure I do not follow pernicious ways,
And guide me in the way that is everlasting."

MY PERSPECTIVES

A SOUND EYE

"The lamp of the body is the eye. It follows that if your eye is sound, your whole body will be filled with sight."

MATTHEW 6:22

The sound eye sees things clearly. The sound eye sees the whole picture. The sound eye allows the light in. The world struggles today with seeing the whole picture, choosing to let in only the light that it chooses. Too often we look through everything with our own lens, seeing only what we want to see, unwilling to find perspective and completeness in our view. We are often blinded by our prejudices and preconceived notions of truth, thereby limiting our views and sacrificing wisdom. Our eyes are damaged. Christ can fix them.

Eyes that cannot see the love of Christ in everything can never be in perfect focus. What we choose to let into our eyes will have an effect on everything about us. We can easily give in to the glare of this world as it overpowers our eyes with things that blur our focus on Christ. The overabundance of images all around us screams for our attention leaving us blind to the simple, absolute truth of Christ. The healthy eye in Christ sees truth and love in all things and at all times. It sees clearly and sharply as it keeps its focus exactly where it needs to be...on Christ.

What comes through the unhealthy eye pollutes the whole body. What comes through the healthy eye penetrates the whole body with love. Don't let this world blur your vision, but instead keep your eyes clearly focused on Christ. See the full spectrum of colors in His love. See how well defined His truth is for each of us. Let our eyes be filled with the images intended for us by Him as we see His fullness and His grace. Let your eyes see Him.

"Let your eyes be fixed ahead,
Your gaze be straight before you."

PROVERBS 4:25

DO NOT JUDGE

"Do not judge, and you will not be judged."

MATTHEW 7:1

Most of us like to put ourselves in the position of judging the actions of others. We compare ourselves to others, judging them by our own standards. We elevate our own self-image and idea of self-importance as we look for chances to pronounce guilt on others. We think that the sins of others far outweigh our own sins as we anxiously try to claim our own righteousness. If we can focus on the faults of others we can ignore or minimize our own failings. This is treacherous ground. We are in no position to judge.

There are no degrees of righteousness. We are either made righteous under the blood of Christ or we are covered in the sin of the world. We like to think that the better we are, the more God loves us. This is not possible. We like to compare ourselves with our brothers and sisters, not by our humility and dependence on God, but by our ego, stature, or place in society. We are competitive, not in our love for God and our need for His grace, but by our need to feel better about ourselves by diminishing others. We want others to live up to our own standards. Instead, we should lean into the real standard of judgment, our faith in God and His grace. Only God can judge.

We like to set the rules, set the boundaries, and be the referee all at the same time. We form immediate opinions based on appearance, failing to see everyone as a created miracle of God. We forget that every life is valued by God, choosing instead to make snap judgments. We get entangled in the opinions of the world, not recognizing that God is the final, ultimate, and worthy judge over all. No other judgment really matters except the judgment of God. Hold Him up with respect and honor.

We are called to a life of love. We are the recipients of God's mercy. He has chosen to show us grace, despite our guilty nature. Leave the judgments to God and live free from the condemnation of sin as a child of God. Treat everyone as God treats you, with grace.

"The following are also taken from the sages:
To show partiality in judgement is not good."

PROVERBS 24:23

RENEW YOUR MIND

"Your mind must be renewed by a spiritual revolution so that you can put on the new self that has been created by God's way, in the goodness and holiness of the truth."

EPHESIANS 4:23

Has your mind experienced a spiritual revolution? Is your life controlled by the influence of your spirit or by your uninspired mind? This verse tells us that our minds need a revolution by the Spirit, a complete turn away from intellect to a dependence on the Spirit. It also tells us that once this Spirit-inspired revolution has dominance in your life, we will obtain our God-created new self! Imagine today's world changed by people whose minds have been renewed by a spiritual revolution and live in the way of God's truth.

Don't be satisfied with a life based on intellect. Instead, nurture your spirit, allowing yourself to be open to the revolution that God has made available to you. Know that God's way is the way of goodness and holiness. Your old mind must be renewed, and it must be renewed in a spiritual way.

We cannot think or rationalize our way to the new life. The new life is one of spiritual dependence, trusting God to transform our old mind into a new, spiritual mind. Priorities will change, focus will change, and dependency will change. Don't forget that God has created the new self you will become, and His promise is goodness and holiness. The truth of God will transform you. Let it happen!

"As no two faces are ever alike, unlike, too, are the hearts of men."

PROVERBS 27:19

ARE YOU THIRSTY?

"If any man is thirsty, let him come to Me! Let the man come and drink who believes in Me!"

JOHN 7:38

Are you thirsty? Thirst is a basic response to a necessity for life. We cannot satisfy thirst by our own doing, but need the refreshment from something outside of ourselves. What are you thirsty for? What basic needs do you have that need to be met? Do you thirst to understand your purpose? Is it a thirst for peace in a world of pressure and conflict? Is it a thirst to end feelings of powerlessness and failure when self-reliance has failed? Is it a desire to find safety and comfort in a time of sorrow? Christ offers satisfaction and relief. He offers to meet your most basic needs at all times, waiting for you to come. He will provide what you cannot, in ways beyond your abilities. When you realize you have weaknesses, He is waiting to support you.

His directions to receive Him are simple and clear: come. Action on our part is commanded and required. A simple act with eternal rewards. Why is it so hard for us to come? It requires faith. It requires trust. It requires humbleness. It requires obedience. It requires the acknowledgment that we continue to fail despite our best efforts and intentions. It means that Christ must become the priority in our life. Only He can satisfy us completely. There is not any rationing of His mercy. He is complete and sufficient to meet all our needs.

Our coming to Him does one more very important thing. It builds a relationship with Him. That relationship builds our dependence and communion with Him. It allows us a chance to honor Christ's sacrificial grace by our commitment and obedience to Him. It changes the way we live, our attitudes, and our priorities. Are you thirsty? Let Him satisfy you completely. Go to Him.

"I love those who love Me;
Those who seek Me eagerly shall find Me."

PROVERBS 8:17

RELY ON SCRIPTURE

"All Scripture is inspired by God and can profitably be used for teaching, for refuting error, for guiding people's lives and teaching them to be holy."

2 TIMOTHY 3:16

Do you depend upon the Scriptures to be your guide in your everyday life? Stop to think about how you decide if something is right or wrong. Do you depend upon the Scriptures to teach you or is the world shaping your intellect? Look at the amount of time and effort people put into searching for truth and self-awareness. Self-help books abound and political pundits try to persuade us. The world is making every effort to tell us how to think and how to live. Do not be fooled by this misinformation.

Everything we need is given to us through God's inspiration in the Scriptures. The holy words, directly inspired by God for our benefit, should be the guide by which we judge all things. If you can accept the fact that the Scriptures hold the God-inspired answers and teachings, you are part way there. Then the next step must be to read them!

Do you spend as much time in the Scriptures as you do reading the newspaper or browsing your computer? What is the percentage of your time spent in the Scriptures versus your time watching TV? Everything you come in contact with every day has an influence on your thinking and attitudes. Be careful not to let the truths in the Scriptures take second place to what the world is telling you. Use the Scriptures to refute the errors of the world and to be your guide on how to live your life. Do not let the world's perceptions determine your actions or concepts of right and wrong. God's Word does not change! Depend upon it on a daily basis to be your guide. Put the truths and teachings of the Scriptures first in your daily thoughts and use them to determine your actions.

Scripture was given to us for our benefit. We all will profit from our commitment to giving the Word priority in our lives. You have influence on everyone that you come into contact with. Will it be influence based on your commitment to the Scriptures or will it be based on your acceptance of the misinformation of the world? The Scriptures are meant to be studied, and the best part of all is they are the truth. Use the Scriptures, depend on the Scriptures, and believe the Scriptures. God has inspired them for you!

"No man is made secure by wickedness,
but nothing shakes the roots of virtuous men."

PROVERBS 12:3

RELIGION

"Nobody must imagine that he is religious while he still goes on deceiving himself and not keeping control over his own tongue; anyone who does this has the wrong idea of religion."

JAMES 1:26

Knowledge without action is empty. Being a Christian involves knowledge, faith, and action. If any of these three parts are missing, we have fallen short of the commands of God.

Obviously we need to know the commandments of God, and we need to strive to continue to gain more knowledge about God and allow ourselves to mature in our knowledge, gaining deeper insights about God. We must also trust the promises of God. We cannot out-think God. But instead, we must trust the promises of God and realize that God reigns over us and accept by faith the knowledge we have of God. The outward expression of our knowledge and faith is our actions, the way we live day to day, moment by moment. Our actions reveal the depth of our understanding and faith. They reveal the level of our reliance on God and His promises. They reveal our willingness to rely on God and our willingness to live a life of love.

Religion should be a way of living, not a base of mere knowledge. Religion is putting our knowledge and faith into daily practice, living His commandments, and allowing our faith to determine our actions.

Examine yourself and see if you consider yourself religious. Does your life reflect the depth of your commitment and faith? Have you given yourself over to God in trust? Do not deceive yourself! Be subject to God's commandments, commit yourself to those commands of faith, and live accordingly.

"To act virtuously and with justice
is more pleasing to God than sacrifice."

PROVERBS 21:3

PSALM 19

Verses 7-9

"The Law of God is perfect,
New life for the soul;
The decree of God is trustworthy,
Wisdom for the simple.
The precepts of God are upright,
Joy for the heart;
The commandment of God is clear,
Light for the eyes.
The fear of God is pure,
Lasting forever;
The judgments of God are true,
Righteous, every one."

MY PERSPECTIVES

TAKE DIRECTION FROM THE SPIRIT

"Since the Spirit is our life, let us be directed by the Spirit. We must stop being conceited, provocative and envious."

GALATIANS 5:25-26

In a time in society where self takes center stage over everything else, is it any wonder that we have pushed God aside? When the mood of the time is to promote personal privilege and demand personal respect, is it any wonder that God has lost societal relevance? In a time where rebellion is championed and glorified, is it any wonder that God is being removed from thought and conversation?

It is no coincidence that the more we promote the importance of our own demands and the more we relegate God to irrelevance that conceit, provocation, and envy flourish. Instant gratification of self has never been more rampant than now as we Twitter, Instagram, Facebook, or whatever our most unfiltered, self-centered thoughts to try to gain acceptance and relevance. Provocation is the name of the game as we try to stir reaction and promote confrontation. Tolerance is demanded, yet rarely given. Compromise is yearned for, yet rarely entertained. Conceit, once despised, is now championed and given multiple platforms to be admired. These conditions are the result of not allowing to be led by what is really important, the Spirit.

For the believer in Christ, the old self and its actions have given way to the new creation we receive through Christ. The Spirit lives in us and can work through us if we will only allow ourselves to be directed. If we are truly guided by the Spirit, we can demonstrate our reliance on the Spirit on a daily, moment-by-moment, basis. We must put our self-indulgent priorities aside and put our faith whole-heartedly in Him. The fruits of this commitment will be easy to see in our attitudes and actions as we interact in this ever-changing world.

The directions in this verse are very straightforward and practical. Stop being conceited! We are not above God! The love of self is one of the biggest obstacles in our relationship to God. It is an obstacle in our relationship with others and an obstacle in our place in society. Put yourself aside and lift up others before yourself.

Stop being provocative! Never be the instigator of someone else's failures or insecurities. Strive to be a peacemaker and not a reason or cause of division. Stop the comments and judgments when you don't know all the facts. Put the best construction on everything and look to de-escalate conflict. Strive for peace over conflict in every situation.

Stop being envious! How much is enough for you? Can you celebrate the good fortunes of others? Can you find contentment and peace with what you have? These are hard questions that when answered will reveal a lot about your relationship with God. It is a gift to be able to appreciate what we have over worry about what we want. There is no peace in a state of envy and there is no thanksgiving to an unsatisfied heart. Find your peace in God and the value of what you have in appreciation toward God. In His Spirit, no matter what you have, your heart will overflow with an abundance of faith.

"The godless man is forever coveting,
The virtuous man gives without ever refusing."

PROVERBS 21:26

DO NOT DRIFT

"We ought then to turn our minds more attentively than before to what we have been taught, so that we do not drift away."

HEBREWS 2:1

Prioritize. What is ***really*** important? What things or circumstances in your daily life will have an eternal impact? In the previous verses to this one, Paul has just been making his case that Christ is greater than any and all things. Christ is the most important thing! There is nothing on this earth that should replace Christ as the number one thing in our lives. When you make a list of the things that are important in your life, is Christ at the top?

Focus. What things in your life have you allowed to get in the way of putting Christ first? Plenty of things and circumstances cry for your attention and seem so important, but are they really important? How many of the things that take your time and energy have eternal repercussions? How many of those things prompt you to look away from Christ and look at yourself? Pay attention to what ***really*** matters: your relationship with Christ.

Habit. We have all experienced lists of intentions that somehow slip away. What happened to the New Year's resolution that somehow is no longer practiced? Taking the easy way once or letting something slip by once...and soon the whole goal is lost. Being a Christian is a way of life, a habit of putting Christ first. It is a mindset to set yourself apart from the crowd and underneath the Lordship of Christ. It is approaching each circumstance of the day as an opportunity for service to God. It is taking the time to be quiet and listen to what God has to say.

Commitment. Being a believer is not an occasional or optional thing. It is an "all in" experience that requires full commitment. We are vehicles of service, gifted by God to reflect the love of Christ. What greater calling can we have? Let us never be the drifter that Paul warns about. Let us be attentive, active, focused children of God.

"He who listens closely to the word shall find happiness;
He who puts his trust in God is blessed."

PROVERBS 16:20

WHILE WE WERE STILL SINNERS

"...but what proves that God loves us is that Christ died for us while we were still sinners."

ROMANS 5:8

Unconditional love. God's love for us is not dependent on who we are, what we do, or even if we love Him. God proved His amazing love through Christ's death for us sinners. There is no limit to His love.

The theme of this verse is seen throughout the Bible. God does not respond in love to us BECAUSE of something we do or do not do. He loves us DESPITE what we do or do not do. Our response to God is because of what He did first, not His reaction to us. Because He did, we should. How difficult it is for us to love someone who doesn't love us. But this is precisely what God did, covering an eternity of sins of a reluctant people through one single sacrificial act. Only God is that kind of love.

Notice that the verse says that "God loves us," not loved us. God continues to love every created soul without hesitation and without question. No matter what circumstance we find ourselves in, God has proven forever that He loves us. That kind of love, which is so hard for us to understand, serves as inspiration and comfort as His compassion covers us. How blessed we are! We have a God that loves us despite our past, despite our current condition, and will love us tomorrow.

It is that kind of love, His sacrificial justifying love, that deserves our response. He has set the example of loving the unloved. He has set the example of sacrifice, loving others at the high cost of the life of His Son. His love is unconditional.

What great comfort and hope this verse gives. God is active in your life. His love can live through each one of us. He is there under any circumstance and He is available to everyone. Let us praise Him for who He is, the author and source of true love. Let us find a way to try to love others in response to His sacrifice. Let us honor Him with our actions, never losing sight that we were created to love.

"He who listens closely to the Word shall find happiness,
he who puts his trust in God is blessed."

PROVERBS 16:20

HIS STRENGTH

"The trials that you have had to bear are no more than people normally have. You can trust God not to let you be tried beyond your strength, and with any trial He will give you a way out of it and the strength to bear it."

1 CORINTHIANS 10:13

What great comfort rests in this verse! God can provide you with all the strength you need, no matter what your own trials might be. This is not an empty promise, but a truth that can play an important part in your life, each and every day.

How many times have you tried to solve your own problems, only to fail? How many times have you looked to yourself to find your answers only to be left empty? There is a way out of your trials, but you have to trust God! He will provide the strength. He will provide the solution. He will provide the peace.

Living in Christ is not about not having problems. Living in Christ is giving yourself up, allowing Christ to be your center and your strength. We are told very plainly that everyone has trials and that they are to be expected. Everyone has their own kind of problems, and yours are no worse than anyone else's. The difference is you, as a Christian, know that God will not exceed the limits of your strength which He provides. He is the answer. He is the way!

When you trust God, the amount of strength you can receive will be beyond your comprehension. You will be able to view your everyday trials in perspective, knowing that nothing can interfere with your trust in God. As your trials attack you today, accept them and look at them as a means of nurturing your dependence on God. Pray, trust, believe, act. God provides you the way. God provides you with strength. As you make your choices, see if they are made with your eyes focused on God or yourself.

Sin is in this world, and you will be attacked. Expect it. God is also in this world and you will be given strength if you trust. Expect it. His victory and peace are yours. Receive it.

"Plans multiply in the human heart,
but the purpose of God stands firm."

PROVERBS 19:21

DO NOT ABUSE HIS GOODNESS

"Or are you abusing His abundant goodness, patience, and tolerance, not realizing that this goodness of God is meant to lead you to repentance."

ROMANS 2:4

His goodness. Everywhere you look God's goodness is evident. His creation reveals His goodness with its beauty and intricacies. His plan of salvation and Christ's sacrifices reveal His kindness and love. His desire to extend His grace to all of us is beyond our understanding. The gift of the Holy Spirit comforts and guides us to live for God's divine purposes. Have you taken the time to acknowledge and appreciate His goodness?

His patience. Time after time we fail, but God continues to give us opportunities for change. His gift of eternal life remains before us despite our self-confident failures. God never forces us, but instead keeps His truths before us, giving us chance after chance to realize the truth of His promises. Free will is His gift and desire, and He waits patiently for our response. How long will you wait?

His tolerance. We fail, we disappoint, we sin, but God remains constant. His grace, promises, and truths remain in place. Our actions isolate us, but

He desires a close, intimate relationship with us. His love is so complete that He sees past our inadequacies and instead sees His created perfection that through His grace we can become. He knows our weaknesses and still desires communion with us. Can you comprehend that level of tolerance?

Why is God so good, patient, and tolerant? It is because He loves us! So what are we to do? Repent and believe! Do we appreciate His deity, or do we strive to elevate ourselves? Do we appreciate the opportunities to serve such an awesome God, or do we spend more time grumbling in circumstances? We were meant to be in a relationship with God. He is good, patient, and tolerant. Will you repent?

"Every word of God is unalloyed,
He is the shield of those who take refuge in Him."

PROVERBS 30:5

REST FOR YOUR SOUL

"Shoulder My yoke and learn from Me, for I am gentle and humble in heart, and you will find rest for your souls."

MATTHEW 11:29

There are times when we cannot find the time to rest. Things come at us faster and faster, demanding our attention, emotion, and time. We are in a constant battle to try to put things into perspective and prioritize what is really important. Where do we put our allegiances? Who do we trust to be the guiding voice in our lives? With so much pointed information coming at us, who can we rely on to be the voice of truth? Jesus has the answer: "learn from me."

When there seems to be no rest in sight, obedience to Jesus will lead the way to peace. When we are overcome with those demanding notoriety and fame, Jesus guides us with His example of humility. When the cries for activism and anger rise around us, we can find comfort in the gentleness of Jesus. Jesus does not lead with anger; He saves with love. When prideful people grab the attention of the day, we can look past those egos to see the value and security of a humble life focused on Jesus.

Sometimes it just seems hard to catch our breath and step back from a world in turmoil. We can so easily get caught up in the anxiety and intensity around us that we lose sight of the fact that we are secure in Jesus. True rest for our soul comes from the assuredness of Jesus, our faith in His resurrection, and our complete commitment to His truth. He is our example. Learn. His spirit is gentle and loving. Follow. His heart is a servant's heart, serving the Father and saving us. Serve.

There is plenty of unrest everywhere we look. People are searching for power and meaning everywhere and are missing the rest and satisfaction that Jesus has already provided. The world is anxious without Jesus. We can be at rest with Him. Take a deep breath and remember His presence, His strength, His peace, and His love. With Him, there is rest and comfort for your soul.

"Better a dry crust and with it peace
Than a house where feast and dispute go together."

PROVERBS 17:1

PSALM 25

Verses 10-14

"All God's paths are love and truth
For those who keep His decrees.
For the sake of Your name, God,
Forgive my guilt, for it is great.
Everyone who fears God
Will be taught the course a man should choose;
His soul will live in prosperity
His children have the land for their own.
The close secret of God belongs to them who fear Him,
His covenant also, to bring them knowledge."

MY PERSPECTIVES

LISTEN AND OBEY

"To listen to the word and not obey is like looking at your own features in a mirror and then after a quick look, going off and immediately forgetting what you looked like."

JAMES 1:23

Listening to the Word is important, but obeying the Word and having the Word be a part of you is much more important. You need to have the Word be an intimate part of yourself, a part that you can recognize. You need to be so familiar and so in touch with the Word that you recognize it immediately and do not forget its nature.

We can all recognize our own image in a mirror because we have seen it so many times. Can you recognize the features of your own obedience to the Word? Is your obedience so natural and consistent that you do not forget the features of your commitment? Your faith and obedience belong to you. Only you can reflect the depth of your commitment.

Commit yourself to taking a long look at the Word and doing all you can to obey it. Be able to be sure of the image you reflect. It is easy to obey when things are going smoothly and we see immediate results, but the depth of your commitment will determine your ability to recognize opportunities to obey the Word even when challenged. The opportunities to obey are all around you, every single day.

Make the Word and your obedience plain to see. Do not just listen! Be obedient! Allow your obedience to become so much a part of your being that it becomes as clear as your own image.

"The path of life is to abide by discipline,
and he who ignores correction goes astray."

PROVERBS 10:17

BE FRIENDS

"Be friends with one another, and kind,
forgiving each other as readily as God forgave you in Christ."

EPHESIANS 4:32

Being a follower of Christ demands that we take on the heart of friendship, kindness, and forgiveness. These qualities are the essence of what it means to put the love of Christ for each of us into action. If we have Christ in us, we will be dear friends, treating others as we wish to be treated. If we have Christ in us, we will be kind to others, happily putting the well-being of others ahead of our own ambitions. If we have Christ in us, we will forgive fully, often, and freely just as we are forgiven in Christ. To be a follower of Christ we must live a life full of compassion.

Being a friend means more than just having an acquaintance with someone. It implies personal interest, personal care, and personal identity. A friend sacrifices and provides. A friend listens with sympathy and acts with empathy. A friend is trusted, dependable, and open. A friend prays.

There are many levels of interactions that we have with those around us, but the most valuable is that of a friend. True friends can be the listening ear, the voice of reason, and the giver of honest advice. A real friend truly cares, willingly doing whatever is necessary to provide comfort and peace.

Christ is your friend. He patiently loves with grace, provides peace and contentment, and listens to your pleas, giving comfort abundantly. He forgave and forgives, time after time, with grace. We have access to the best friend ever, Christ, through faith. With Him in us, we are free to be that same kind of friend to all those around us. Be a friend and let the light of Christ flow through you to show His love to everyone. Be kind and forgive with passion, purpose, and integrity.

"Fragrant oil gladdens the heart,
Friendship's sweetness comforts the soul."

PROVERBS 27:9

DO YOU BELIEVE HE CAN?

"And when Jesus reached the house the blind men came up with Him and He said to them, 'Do you believe I can do this?' They said, 'Sir, we do'."

MATTHEW 9:28

We pray for things that we need, but do we pray with an expectation of the answer? We pray for situations to change, but do we look for the hand of God in the answer? Is praying for a miracle a nice thing to do, or a plea for the direct hand of God to have personal influence? I have to ask myself over and over again, "Do I really believe Jesus can do this?" I believe in God, but tend to minimize His power. I look to God, but end up trusting myself instead. I pray for peace and rest, but never focus on the source of that peace and rest. Do I believe…really believe…that He can answer prayer and direct events?

It seems like I go to Jesus when I am out of other options, having failed myself and perceiving myself as a victim of circumstance rather than a victor in Him. I end up trusting myself to manufacture a miracle in my life rather than trusting God to provide, care, and lead me to what is important. I become frustrated when I live a life based on my personal timetable rather than resting in the glory and grace of Jesus. More than anything I would like to join those blind men with an emphatic "YES, I BELIEVE YOU CAN," throwing my full trust and dependence on Jesus. But it seems like I get in the way, finding that my belief is dependent upon repetitive proof rather than trust and faith. Do I really believe?

If God is God, He can do anything. He has chosen to love me, just as I am. He has chosen me to be a vehicle to demonstrate His mercy, His compassion, and His love. I can trust God because He has never failed, never changed, and always loves. I can join those blind men to declare, "YES, I DO BELIEVE YOU CAN," because God is God. I pray that I look at everything through the lens of being a child of God, seeing opportunities to love where I can, demonstrating trust in Him always, and knowing that He is always there for me. I pray that I look outside of myself and inside my heart, to feel His constant presence and His guidance in my life. Do I believe He can do this? Yes.

"A man's heart plans out his way,
But it is God who makes his steps secure."

PROVERBS 16:9

AND THEY LEFT AT ONCE

"And they left their nets at once and followed Him."

MATTHEW 4:20

What holds us back from this type of commitment? It took only one sentence from Jesus to get a one hundred percent response from Peter and Andrew. There was no hesitation and no debate. They didn't ask for a long list of reasons or promises. They simply committed. In an instant, they were ready to leave the world they knew behind and follow Jesus.

Ask yourself if you have the same type of commitment and open mind that Peter and Andrew had. What would we be looking for in today's world if we were presented with the same opportunities? Would we have a list of questions? Would we need some kind of guarantee?

Jesus didn't provide Peter and Andrew with a list of reasons or explanations to try to convince them to follow Him. Jesus didn't offer them a better pay package or more vacation, a life free from pain, or financial independence. What He gave them was an opportunity for a relationship with Him. He offered a new life in Christ. He offered to be fishers of men. Included in this new life would be the opportunity for relationship with others, sharing the news of Christ's plan for salvation. They were given the opportunity to participate in changing lives and eternity for the world.

In one sentence, Jesus was able to communicate the importance of His invitation to them, and in an instant, they responded. We are no different than Peter and Andrew, going about our everyday lives thinking that what we are doing is important. What we need to learn from Peter and Andrew is more about response to an opportunity than anything else. Their willingness to change their lives and be committed followers of Christ gives us an example of true Christianity. Their response allowed simple fishermen to become world changers.

How would you respond in the same situation? Would your response be an immediate, "Yes, Lord," or a request for more information? Would we be able to put the kind of faith and trust that Peter and Andrew had into a committed response? For Peter and Andrew there was no ambivalence and no second-guessing. Their response revealed a trust and faith that may be hard for us to understand, yet speaks so loudly to the lordship of Jesus. How passionate He must have been. How convincing He must have been. How overwhelming His presence must have been. The same opportunities are there for us, waiting for a response of commitment. What is holding you back?

"Ear that hears, eye that sees,
God has made both of these."

PROVERBS 20:12

HE IS REAL

"Something which has existed since the beginning, that we have heard, and we have seen with our own eyes; that we have watched and touched with our hands: The Word who is life—this is our subject."

1 JOHN 1:1

Christ fulfills the intimacy of the Word. The Word is alive. They are not merely words on a page, the Word is something that stimulates all of our senses. We see it. We can touch it. It penetrates our soul down to its essence and changes both our lives here on earth and our eternity. His Word is something that we were meant not just to read, but to experience and become part of. The Word speaks to the nature of God and our relationship with Him. He has always existed and we have always been part of His plan. He has provided us with a living testimony of His Godship, and His Word speaks to us each and every time we read it. It contains more than words. It is power. It is strength. It is intimacy with God.

Every human condition is captured in the Word, and His understanding and grace are the purest form of peace we can ever experience. His warnings and corrections, which are revealed in His Word, give us a compass to guide us and emphasize our need for commitment to Him. His sacrifice and love that is revealed in His Word give us hope and trust that ours will be an eternity spent with Him. How real is the Word to you? To John, it was absolutely part of his being. It was something marvelous, miraculous, and beyond his understanding, yet at the same time something real and practical in his life. To John, nothing could have been more intimate and powerful in his life. Do you feel that same type of connection? Is the Word so real to you that you feel its power? The Word **IS** life. Let it be real and powerful in you.

"From everlasting I was firmly set,
From the beginning before earth came into being."

PROVERBS 8:23

EVERYONE

"You see, God's grace has been revealed, and it has made salvation possible for the whole human race..."

TITUS 2:11

This verse is the Good News for all of us. God has chosen to include every soul in His plan for salvation! In a time in history where we tend to focus on the differences among people, this verse speaks to the commonality of the human race. God does not play favorites. Christ's life, death, and resurrection were for all! Differences make no difference in the eyes of God—rich or poor, man or woman, Jew or Gentile.

It is an all too human thing for us to try to categorize people, making immediate presumptions because of human traits, heritage, and stature. We put up barriers that keep people apart, desperately trying to measure ourselves against others. It is with a sense of egotism that some try desperately to elevate themselves, while it is with a sense of despair that others give in to a sense of unworthiness. Neither position is what God's grace declares.

While we may come from different backgrounds, economic conditions, or may be at different stages in our lives, the grace of God gives us the common bond that will make a difference in eternity. If God's salvation is for everyone, how dare we not treat others as equal recipients of grace? All believers are

EQUAL heirs with Christ in salvation. All believers are EQUAL recipients of the justification and atonement that come from Christ. All believers are EQUAL recipients of the sanctification that comes from the blood of Christ.

With this in mind, why is it so hard to find commonality rather than difference among people? May we all be children of God who see His hand in everyone. We have an opportunity every day to set a different standard, a standard of respect and honor to all God's children. Set the media blitz aside and listen instead to the heart of God. Celebrate our commonality in God and let differences be opportunities to encourage understanding. If God has chosen to be inclusive, why not us as well?

Never let others tell us that we need to meet some kind of human standard to receive salvation that will fail if we do not measure up. We sinners are included in God's grace! Do not let people pigeonhole us as individuals needing to meet human expectations. Who are you really as a believer? A child of God? A co-heir with Christ to salvation? A person whom God loves? Have faith and never lose heart.

"To be afraid of men is a snare,
He who puts his trust in God is secure."

PROVERBS 29:25

PSALM 4

Verses 1,3

"God, guardian of my rights,
You answer when I call,
When I am in trouble,
You come to my relief;
Now be good to me and hear my prayer."
"Know this, God works wonders for those He loves,
God hears me when I call to him."

MY PERSPECTIVES

LIVE BY TRUTH

"But the man who lives by the truth comes out into the light, so that it may be plainly seen that what he does is done in God."

JOHN 3:21

What a world this would be if everyone lived by truth! Imagine a world free of posturing, misguided intentions, and ill motives. What a world this would be!

We have to ask ourselves, what is truth? Truth is always consistent with God. Since truth is part of the nature of God, He cannot be separated from it. Truth is always in harmony with the mind of God and is always within His will. Truth is part of God's creation and His declarations of reality make His Truth absolute and everlasting. God is Truth.

Living in truth means that we live a life centered on God. It means living a life of transparency, letting all facets of our life reflect the peace and joy we have because of His grace. It means living with assurance and trust in God, knowing that His promises are real and reliable. Above all, it means living a life based on His love for us. We are free to love abundantly, just as He abundantly loves us. God is real. God is love. God is truth.

All who live in the truth have the opportunity to be witnesses for the love of God. A gracious act by us serves to reveal His grace. Generosity on our part lets people see the generosity of God. Any loving act by us lets the love of God shine. We need to always be bold in our commitment to live by the truth of God, doing our best to remain faithful and committed to His honesty and graciousness.

In a time where people are searching for truth, we have the opportunity to let the love of God be plainly seen if we stay in the light of His truth. Commit to being different, assured, and committed. Trust in the absolute truth of His love and grace. Let His light shine through you. What an example you can be!

"The path of the virtuous is like the light of dawn,
Its brightness growing to the fullness of day."

PROVERBS 4:4

BE WORTHY OF HIS TRUST

"People must think of us as Christ's servants, stewards entrusted with the mysteries of God. What is expected of stewards is that each one should be found worthy of His trust."

1 CORINTHIANS 4:1-2

Trust. It is a word that has a tremendous impact. So many traits make up the character of trust. Consistency. Honor. Reliability. Truth. Honesty. Dependability. Do you consider yourself a servant of Christ? Are you a good steward of the gifts that He has given you? If so, how many of the traits that describe trust can be found in your character?

Our world is full of secularism, half-truths, and no absolutes. The constant battle goes on between what the world expects and directs with the moral standards that God places in our hearts. We have been entrusted as Christians with the mysteries of God. How can we be expected to be considered good stewards of these mysteries if we are not trustworthy? We must embody the traits of the Spirit. When we speak, others must know it is the truth. They must know by our character that they can depend on what we say because we consistently speak the truth. There must be no hypocrisy in us. We cannot say one thing by the Spirit, yet act another way for the world.

Of course we will fail at times, but good stewards of God's mysteries must keep His Spirit alive inside themselves, striving to use every worldly situation as an opportunity to make God's truths more evident.

Being a Christian is a wonderful obligation. Will you be found worthy of His trust? Will people see your actions and know they come from a godly perspective? Would the word "servant" properly describe you? Let the traits of trust become part of you with God's help. Pray that you would be trusted to be considered worthy of the trust of others. You have been entrusted with the mysteries of God. Speak the truth, earn trust, and have others know they can depend on you to reveal to them true stewardship. It is what God expects!

"So that your trust may be in God,
Today I propose to make your way known to you."

PROVERBS 22:19

DO NOT DELUDE YOURSELF

"Don't delude yourself into thinking God can be cheated: where a man sows, there he reaps; if he sows in the field of self-indulgence he will get a harvest of corruption out of it; if he sows in the field of the Spirit, he will get from it a harvest of eternal life."

GALATIANS 6:6

There is no way to fool God. Where do we put our faith? Is it in ourselves or is it in the Spirit? The one thing we cannot do is put ourselves first and somehow think that our reward will still be that of the promises of the Spirit. We cannot reap the harvest of eternal life when we depend solely on ourselves.

Self-reliance surely leads to the harvest of corruption. Without reliance on the Spirit we are destined to a life filled only with unholy corruption. How do we get ourselves out of the field of self-indulgence and into the field of the Spirit? First of all, we need to come to the realization that we do not have the ability to make our own road to eternal life. Left to our own abilities, we cannot escape the debts that our sins have accumulated. Time after time we will fall short.

Obtaining perfection is impossible. This verse tells us that our self-indulgence will only bring a life of corruption. It is only by identifying with and staying available to the Spirit that we can reap a different harvest. We need to spend our time in the field of the Spirit, committing ourselves to a life of dependence, not on ourselves, but on the promises and power for the Spirit. Only then will we reap the heavenly harvest.

We can fool ourselves, but we cannot fool God. Our hearts will determine which field we sow in. Commit yourself to the field of the Spirit and the harvest of eternal life will be yours.

"The contrary heart does not find happiness,
the deceitful tongue falls into distress."

PROVERBS 17:20

ALL

Jesus said, "You must love the Lord your God with all your heart, with all your soul, and with all your mind. This is the greatest and first commandment."

MATTHEW 22:37-39

All. Jesus did not say a portion, occasionally, or with reservation. He said all. Does this describe your commitment to the Lord your God? Every one of us falls short of this greatest and first commandment. What do you put first? Who do you put first?

It is our commitment to obedience to this commandment that sets the pattern for our lives. Honoring this commandment determines our motivations and purity of action. It becomes the reason for our being and gives meaning to our lives.

This is a commandment that leaves no room for rationalization or situational obedience. God is God. It is with our entire being that we are commanded to commit ourselves to Him. There is no middle ground.

What are the consequences of failure to follow this commandment? Our selfishness impedes our reliance and trust in Him. Our pride elevates our self-image to a level of self-importance that fails time and time again to meet our expectations. Our eternal view is pushed aside, and we focus on the immediate wants of our flesh to satisfy ourselves, only to feel empty and unfulfilled. Peace eludes us. Have you taken the time to see what is taking your "all?"

Where is the hope? God's commandment places Him first. It is in Him that our perspectives change, our hearts fill with compassion, and we happily take on the role of servants. It is only by being in relationship with Him that we can put things in their proper perspective and begin to live eternally now. God wants every part of our actions, thoughts, and emotions. He deserves our "all." What is stopping you? Why are you holding anything back? He is the answer, and He holds out His gift of peace to each of us. The greatest commandment is clear and straightforward. Will you obey?

"Commend what you do to God,
And your plans will find achievement."

PROVERBS 16:3

HIS CHILDREN

"Yet in fact He is not far from any of us, since it is in Him that we live, and move, and exist, as indeed some of your own writers have said: 'We are all His children'."

ACTS 17:28

We are created beings, formed individually and bestowed with gifts from God. Our whole existence can never be apart from Him. We have been given our bodies to function in this world and our existence as a form cannot be separated from Him. We are each given emotions and feelings so that we can interact with those around us with meaning. We can exhibit care, compassion, and love to those around us. We can feel pain and joy, sorrow and gladness. We are blessed to experience the life around us. We are gifted with the ability to learn and reason, to comprehend and question. We can see outside of our own existence and acknowledge that there is more to life than just being. We are the living evidence of the love of God. We are given the capacity to know there is a God and that He deserves our worship, praise, and honor. We are so fortunate to be able to see, feel, and experience the love of God.

Whether we believe it or not, it does not change the fact that God is in everything, and we can see it if we want to look. God is in the compassion we show when meeting the needs of others. God is in the sunrise and sunset that we enjoy. God is in the love a mother has for her newborn child. God is in the heart of the child caring for their aging parent. God is in friendship. God is in service. God is in love.

Wouldn't this be a different world if we all tried to see God in every situation? Wouldn't you treat others differently if you saw God in them instead of their shortcomings? Wouldn't we appreciate the world around us as we recognize it as a created gift from God and our responsibilities to preserve it? What are you waiting for? Why not see God everywhere?

All of us are under God's care and we should never forget that we are all equally loved. His plan for salvation was for an entire world, including the worst of us and despite the worst in us. It is through faith in Jesus Christ that we can bind ourselves together with Him and call ourselves children of God and heirs with Christ. We are His, if we let ourselves be taken. What are you waiting for?

Look at this world with new eyes, focused squarely on God. See the love of God in everything, everywhere, always. Know that God has compassion on all His children and He will never leave us. Appreciate what God has done for you and live with a new vision of yourself and others, seeing God.

As a child of God, recognize His position and power. Go to Him when you need Him. Give Him the honor and worship that He deserves. Be thankful, be humble, and rest in Him. With the same love that He created you, He has given you a future with Him. Find Him wherever you are.

"For God Himself is giver of wisdom,
From His mouth issue knowledge and discernment."

PROVERBS 2:6

PAY BACK WITH A BLESSING

"Never pay back one wrong with another; instead, pay back with a blessing. That is what you are called to do, so that you inherit a blessing yourself."

1 PETER 3:9

Do you want to set yourself apart from the world as a Christian? Do you want to demonstrate the peace of Christ to a world locked in conflict? Do you want to turn a world where retaliation is expected upside down? Do you want to be the one who stops anger and promotes the kindness of Christ instead? This verse tells us how to accomplish these goals. Always pay back others with a blessing.

This verse also tells us some truths that are too often neglected in our present world. Love is stronger than hate. Compassion has power over selfishness. Caring is more fulfilling than selfishness. Peace will always win over aggression. A heart filled with Christ can change everything. Christ calls us specifically to mirror His peace in every situation. It is expected. It is always right. It is the character of Christ. This verse also tells us to not just ignore a wrong, but pay it back with a blessing. It is up to us as Christians to go the extra mile, to go out of our way to reveal the heart of Christ in every situation. If someone is wrong, pray for them. If someone lets you down, love them in return. If someone speaks badly about you, speak well of them. If someone disappoints you, embrace compassion.

There is no penalty for being kind. There is only a blessing, to both the giver and the receiver. Giving a blessing when one is not deserved shows strength, not weakness. Retaliation is not the path of the believer. The proof of our blessing from Christ is our willingness and desire to bless others. It is what we are expected to do in Christ Jesus.

Words have power both negatively and positively. Actions speak louder than words. Make the commitment to bless both with words and actions and you will be doing the will of God. Being a blessing to others is not what the world expects, but it is what God has called every believer to put into practice.

"Do not say, 'I will repay evil';
Put your hope in God and He will keep you safe."

PROVERBS 20:22

PSALM 150

"Alleluia!
Praise God in His temple on earth,
Praise Him in His temple in heaven,
Praise Him for His mighty achievements,
Praise Him for His transcendent greatness!
Praise Him with blasts of the trumpet,
Praise Him with lyre and harp,
Praise Him with drums and dancing,
Praise Him with strings and reeds,
Praise Him with clashing cymbals,
Praise Him with clanging cymbals,
Let everything that breathes praise God!
Alleluia!"

MY PERSPECTIVES

ENOUGH TALK

"My children, our love is not to be just words or mere talk, but something real and active..."

1 JOHN 3:18

So often things are easy to say but difficult to do. It is great to have an opinion, but much harder to put that opinion into action. It is easy to talk about being a follower of Christ, but often much more difficult to reveal our dedication to Him by showing love. The evidence of how we really feel is most often revealed in how we live. The true believer in Christ is obligated to put that faith into action, bringing His Spirit alive in all that he does.

Today we are bombarded with facts and opinions, choices and pathways, philosophies and plans. This age of communication carries with it an essential problem: it lacks the teeth of action. It is easy for the Christian to fall into the same pit of inaction. We can give opinions, judge, and criticize all while failing to make our faith in Christ something real and alive. Faith must dictate how we live and interact with a society in desperate need of faith in action. We speak of the love of Christ, yet too often fail to love His creation. We speak of Christ saving sinners, yet too often spend more time judging and setting ourselves apart from those who do not meet our standards. We speak of the generosity of God, yet turn our heads away from meeting the needs of others. Too much talk and not enough action.

We need to look no further than Christ Himself when it comes to love revealed in a real and active way. Christ taught to love...and came to earth to save. Christ taught humility and bore the sins of us all. Christ talked of sacrifice and died on a cross as the ultimate sacrifice. Christ talked of priorities and lived a life of obedience to the Father. Christ lived the perfect life, actively pursuing peace and comfort to all who put their trust in Him. Forgiveness... through His blood. Eternal life....through sharing His broken body. Peace... through His power.

What sets us apart as a Christian more completely, the way we talk or what we do? Does our faith reveal itself as real by what we say or by what we do? What reveals the true heart of the believer more correctly, words or action? This verse is a call to action, to put the true faith in Christ into real terms to those around us. We are called to make our faith part of the way we not just think, but the way we live. Every day we have opportunities all around us to live a life of love. There is a chance to show compassion everywhere. There is a chance to be humble in conflict, truthful in stress, and faithful to Christ. There is always the opportunity to show the love of Christ for no other reason than because He first loved us. Know Christ. Trust Christ. Believe Christ. Live Christ.

"Let God be pleased with a man's way of life
And he makes his very enemies into friends."

PROVERBS 16:7

EACH DAY

"So do not worry about tomorrow: tomorrow will take care of itself. Each day has enough trouble of its own."

MATTHEW 6:34

Worry. Worry. Worry. Sometimes it seems that that is all that we do. Everywhere you look there seems to be bad news, natural disasters, and conflicts dominating the media. There are deadlines to meet, personalities to contend with, and everyday pressures and stresses to deal with. Sometimes it seems as if our futures are out of our control, and we fill our minds with a series of "what-if" questions and doubts.

The good news is that there really is someone in control, God. The acceptance of that fact is the first step toward putting worry in its place. It isn't easy to admit, but no matter how important you think you are, you are not in control of nearly as many situations as you think.

So the basic question becomes: whom do you trust? If you truly trust God, then there is no need to worry. God sees the big picture and can use the perceived problems of each day for His purposes. We, on the other hand, see only a few facts in front of us and try desperately to manipulate them to our immediate benefit. Worry is a direct effect of trying to place ourselves in the position of control.

Has worrying ever changed the future? What would happen if you changed your attitude and looked at the unknowns of the future as opportunities? What would happen if you truly believed that those same unknowns were part of God's plan? There is no doubt that each day has enough troubles of its own, but we only make them worse by taking ownership of those troubles. We multiply them over and over again when we worry about those troubles and the potential for more troubles in the future.

God promises to take care of us, even if there are struggles in our lives. If you trust those promises, worry will not be an issue. Instead, each day will be looked at as a fresh set of circumstances giving us a chance to reveal the Christian traits of perseverance, trust, humility, and love. Trust God to provide for all your needs today, tomorrow, and in eternity. Take each day as it comes and respond to it as a good steward of the gifts that God has given you. Each day is a gift. Enjoy it.

"To be afraid of men is a snare,
He who puts his trust in God is secure."

PROVERBS 29:25

WHERE IS MY MIRACLE?

"...and He could work no miracle there, though He cured a few sick people by laying His hands on them. He was amazed at their lack of faith."

MARK 6:5-6

Jesus was always willing to act lovingly and mercifully in the lives of all those around Him, but those gifts could not be received without faith. Jesus had proven Himself time and time again, teaching with authority and healing with compassion, yet there were those that still did not believe. No amount of evidence would soften their hardened hearts. Their unbelief kept the miracles of Jesus away. I need to ask myself if my unbelief is getting in the way of what He intends to give me.

There is a big difference between believing there is God and believing in God. God is not something "out there," He is someone "in here." He does not need to continually prove Himself to me, I need to show my continual faith in Him. There are times when I trust myself instead of trusting Jesus. There are times when I need a miracle yet do not trust in the way that He provides. I keep Him at arm's length, using Him as my last option when all else has failed. I may be missing my miracle.

When I do not have faith, doubt and skepticism are never far behind. When I do not have faith, I fail miserably trying desperately to create my own miracle. When I do not have faith, I have broken the relationship that could be mine with Jesus. With faith, all things are possible in Him. With faith, I know that all things happen for my good as He provides His peace and contentment in my life. With faith, I can trust in something bigger, more powerful, and more loving than myself as He shows His mercy and is able to soften my heart. Alone, miracles are not possible. Miracles are His gift. Stay persistent in your faith in Jesus, and enjoy His power in your life. There may be a miracle right around the corner.

"Trust wholeheartedly in God,
Put no faith in your own perception."

PROVERBS 3:5

DO NOT LIMIT YOURSELF

"It is death to limit oneself to what is unspiritual; life and peace can only come with concern for the spiritual."

ROMANS 8:6

Where is peace, contentment, and quality of life? The tragedy of humanity is we look to secular solutions which only spiritual things can solve. Too often we find a way to separate our spirituality from everyday life. Politics and business are divorced from God. Tolerance and apathy condone practices as acceptable when they are really unspiritual. Rationalization and circumstantial attitudes move us further away from spiritual truth.

This verse could not be any clearer about the consequences of our choices: life or death. Spiritual or unspiritual. Godly or worldly. The choice is ours and the outcomes are eternal. Spirituality is about obedience, trust, and humility. Spirituality is about commitment, wholeness, and peace. Life and peace are products of a soul committed to spiritual things. They are relational in nature and recognize the higher power and calling of God. They recognize that true peace can only come from opening ourselves to the spiritual nature of God and by expecting through faith that God will provide all that we need to have a life of peaceful service.

Time after time the temptation and promises of the world fail. More and more material things do not satisfy and our efforts to control our lives are unsuccessful. Only by admitting that God is in control and that truly important, lasting things in life are spiritual can we expect to find true peace. God is God, and He will provide. Anxiety and worrying are things of this world, not of God. Greed and materialism get in the way of our reliance and trust in God. Conceit and pride only set us up for failure. Do not limit yourself by relying on unspiritual things.

The Spirit is the source of a life full of happiness and contentment that is not dependent on circumstances. Your choice is a way of life, not a way out of hardships or difficulties. Choose the spiritual, and enjoy the life of peace that God has waiting for you. He will provide.

"The wise man sees evil coming and avoids it,
The fool is rash and presumptuous."

PROVERBS 14:16

WHOSE SIDE ARE YOU ON?

"He who is not with me is against me;
and he who does not gather with me scatters."

LUKE 11:23

There is no compromise. There is no debate between us and God as to who is right and who is in charge. We try to make it so difficult with our rationalizations and reasoning, yet it cannot be clearer. We must not only be one hundred percent dedicated to God, but also do everything we can to gather more to Him as well.

We cannot choose when and where we will follow Him and still consider ourselves His child. This verse is about commitment, complete commitment. It is about trust and relationship with God. It is about our motivations and allegiances. Are you with Him? Do you gather? Anything short of these descriptions fails. Anything short of these descriptions is harmful. Anything short of these descriptions takes us out of our relationship with God.

It is time to declare yourself. You can stand with Him or away from Him, but you cannot stand in both places. To stand with Him puts God at your center and directs your actions to be based on dependence on Him. To stand on your own means your motives are self-serving and you depend on yourself.

Dependence or independence. Obedience or self-reliance. Humility or pride. Generosity or selfishness. A witness for Him or a witness against Him. It is a bold decision that requires conviction, courage, and commitment. It is the most important decision we can make in our lives with eternal ramifications.

Consider the two thieves hanging on each side of Christ at His crucifixion. One was with Him, the other against. One was promised paradise with God while the other was not. There was no middle ground for them, and there is no middle ground for us. Which one do you identify with? Which side of the cross will you declare? Choose Him.

"For the errors of the ignorant lead to their destruction,
And the complacency of fools work to their or ruin.
But whoever listens to me may live secure,
He will have quiet, fearing no mischance."

PROVERBS 1:32-33

BEWARE THE MISCHIEF MAKERS

"'At the end time,' they told you 'there are going to be people who sneer at religion and follow nothing but their own desires for wickedness. These unspiritual and selfish people are nothing but mischief-makers.'"

JUDE 18-19

Day by day the world is developing mischief-makers. These people make it their objective to fulfill their own desires. Religion is being pushed into the background as people put themselves before God. Self-gratification is held as a more desirable goal, lowering sacrifice, worship, and humility to a status that is mocked. The pursuit of earthly riches finds little time for religion. Where have we gone wrong? How did everything get turned upside down?

Mischief-makers are flourishing! In this verse we are reminded what the Apostles were warning us about. We now live in a world where the emphasis is on getting, not giving. Oh how foolish we are. Religion is not to be sneered at, but embraced. Desires are not to be for our own wicked ways, but for love. We have been given spiritual gifts but seem to let the unspiritual influence us. Selfishness is a manifestation of our lack of trust and contentment.

Where do you place yourself on the selfishness scale? Is your faith capable of withstanding the attacks by the mischief-makers? Will you allow their sneers to break your bonds with God? Now is the time for perseverance and a total commitment to faith. The prediction of the Apostles is right in front of our eyes. The end time is nearing and it is important that we realize where our hearts need to be. The mischief-makers cannot change the promises of God or diminish the sacrifices of Christ. Hold fast to your religion and follow the desire of God, not man. Look around, open your eyes. As every day passes, it is essential that we deepen our reliance on one thing, the grace of God. We are His. Dedicate yourself to love, not mischief. Your renewal is a gift that is yours for the believing.

"The godless is forever coveting,
the virtuous man gives without ever refusing."

PROVERBS 21:26

PSALM 100

"Acclaim God, all the earth, serve God gladly,
Come into His presence with songs of joy!
Know that He, God, is God,
He made us and we belong to Him,
We are His people, the flock that He pastures.
Walk through His porticos giving thanks,
Enter His courts praising Him,
Give thanks to Him, bless His name!
Yes, God is good,
His love is everlasting,
His faithfulness endures from age to age."

MY PERSPECTIVES

A DEEP RELATIONSHIP

"For I told you, if your virtue goes no deeper than that of the scribe and the Pharisees, you will never get into the kingdom of heaven."

MATTHEW 5:20

Christ wants a relationship rather than a ritual. Christ wants pure intentions rather than obligation. Christ wants pure motivations rather than self-serving reasoning. We need to look at our life and see if it is a witness to the personal relationship that we have with Christ. Too often decisions are based on ritual, custom, or legalism when instead they should be based on love, compassion, and service.

Relationship with Christ is based on dependence and trust, not regulation and rules. It is that relationship that determines our motivations and actions. Our reasoning needs to be based on meeting the needs of others and never letting legalism get in the way of others coming to Christ. Christ wants a deep, personal relationship with each of us. He does not want a casual friendship or merely an acknowledgment of His existence. He wants all that we are. That type of deep relationship witnesses for Christ continually, in all circumstances. We were not called to set ourselves apart from others, but instead to involve our lives and Christian values into our society. We were not called to judge others and set the standards for their behavior, but instead to reveal Christ's love to all we come in contact with.

Religion should never get in the way of the Great Commission. Too often we honor one way of doing things and our religious customs more than we honor the intentions of our Lord and Savior. Living daily in a deep relationship with Christ is more important than any ritual or rule. Christ challenged the Pharisee's ideas of right and wrong and showed them that humility, compassion, and humbleness were the keys to being sons of God. He pointed out their self-righteousness and spoke of its dangers. He made clear that we have all sinned. As a result, each of us needs forgiveness and deep relationship with Him.

How deep is your life in Christ? Make a relationship with Him your highest priority.

"Trust wholeheartedly in God
Put no faith in your own perception."

PROVERBS 3:5

HIS VICTORY

"...so that by His death He could take away all the power of the devil, who had power over death, and set free all those who had been held in slavery all their lives by the fear of death."

HEBREWS 2:14-15

Victory! Freedom! Triumph! A single sacrifice has saved us from the fear and power of the devil. No other single act could have changed the history of mankind. With Christ's sacrifice came a victory so profound we never would have achieved it alone.

With Christ's sacrifice came freedom. We are no longer bound by fear. We are now empowered to be partners in His victory and can share in His victory. Our lives will never be the same! Death is no longer a boundary for us and we no longer need to live our lives as if we have an end. Death does not contain us any longer. Christ has taken away the power and limits of death.

Do you live your life knowing that much more awaits you after death? Are you living for eternity? This verse leaves no doubt who is in charge of your eternity. We know where the true power rests. It rests solely with God! This verse assures us of the infinite power of God. Not only did He conquer death, but by His sacrificial gift took away all the power of the devil.

God is great, God is powerful, and God is in charge. God's power has taken all the restraints off of our lives and we are free to live as His children knowing that this world cannot take away the precious relationship we have with God.

God has given this all to us as a gift, a gift which we receive by believing. The life of a believer is characterized by trust, faith, and acceptance. Take hold of the gift that God holds in front of you. Enjoy the freedom that comes from trusting God. Live as a devoted follower of God, full of the knowledge of what God has done for you. Know that God has triumphed and that no longer can anything keep you from God. We have nothing to fear, either in life or death. Receive the prize. God has set you free, so live with joy. God has conquered both death and fear. You are free!

"The name of God is a strong tower;
the virtuous man runs to it and is secure."

PROVERBS 18:10

WHERE IS YOUR FAITH?

"He said to them, 'Where is your faith?' They were awestruck and astonished and said to one another, 'Who can this be, that gives orders even to winds and waves and they obey him?'"

LUKE 8:25

Sometimes God calms the storms around you. Sometimes God lets the storms go on and challenges you. Our faith in Him can find the love of God in either option. It is too easy to look at problems as external forces when sometimes the peace we are looking for is inside of ourselves. We get caught up thinking if only things were different then I would be at peace. If only, if only, if only. As soon as, as soon as, as soon as. This attitude makes us ask a simple, yet ultimately the most important, question. Where is your faith?

The disciples were being tossed about by the winds and waves of the storm on the lake. We are all being tossed about by the winds and waves of a sinful world. The disciples felt they were going to go down in the lake and be swallowed by its power. We so often feel helpless and powerless to chart our own course in the surge and pull of the world around us. The disciples knew their hope for survival was dependent on Jesus. Where is your hope for survival? Where is your faith?

Jesus did two things in the moment. He showed His power over the circumstance, and He changed hearts. The disciples were awestruck and astonished when they relied on Jesus. When was the last time you were awestruck by Jesus? Have you given Him the chance to change your heart or do you insist that the circumstances change first? In extreme peril, the disciples went to their Master. In a moment of fear, they looked to Jesus to save them. At a time when the disciples were powerless, they ran to the ultimate power, Jesus. Jesus did not rebuke the disciples. He rebuked the wind. He calmed the waters and the hearts of the disciples. He can calm our hearts as well. Where is your faith?

In our lives, the circumstances may seem rough and powerful, but we have a Lord who is more. His power saves, His power calms, and His power overwhelms. Let Jesus astonish you. Let Jesus awe you. Let Jesus be your focus. Instead of being paralyzed by circumstances, live at peace and in freedom because your faith is in Him. When Jesus asks you, 'Where is your faith?' be able to assuredly say, 'My faith is in you. Thank you for saving me.'

"In every course you take, have Him in mind:
He will see that your paths are smooth."

PROVERBS 3:6

THE HABIT OF OBEDIENCE

"Do not behave in the way that you liked before you learnt the truth; make a habit of obedience."

1 PETER 1:14

The truth. All believers are new creatures in Christ. But do you live in surety of this?

1. Does God come first in every way? Is God your priority, foundation, and at the heart of every decision and action?
2. Can you honestly say that godly decisions are made before personal decisions?
3. Do you recognize the power and supremacy of God?
4. Do you accept that God expects and deserves obedience to Him?
5. Do you recognize the importance of family and do all you can to bring harmony?
6. Do you honor all life and do your best to nourish relationships?
7. Can you separate yourself from the ways of the world?
8. Can you treat everyone in an honest, humble fashion with truth as the foundation?
9. Can you find happiness in the success of others and celebrate their gifts?

10. Can you find contentment with what you have and share with those in need, leaving selfishness behind?

Habits are built when we give importance to their value. What can be of greater value than to be a new creature in Christ? Obedience is the outward sign that we acknowledge the authority of God. We do not obey to try to earn salvation, but instead obey because He first loved us. We are His children, heirs with Christ in the gift of salvation. Living for Christ needs to be our way of life, the underpinning of our character. Live the new way and in happy obedience to Jesus.

"To turn from evil is the way of honest men;
He keeps his life safe who watches where he goes."

PROVERBS 16:17

HEART AND TREASURE

"For where your treasure is, there will your heart be also."

MATTHEW 6:21

What is important to you? What do you focus on? How do you spend your time? What dominates your attention? The answers to these questions will reveal what you consider your treasure. We may not like the answers, but they uncover our goals, priorities, and character. They uncover what we are willing to sacrifice and cannot be separated from our heart. Is God your treasure, or do you worry more about worldly gains and aspirations? Is God your treasure, or is your faith given importance only for our own benefit? Is God your treasure, or does selfishness and ego demand the bulk of your time? Is God your treasure, or do you rely on yourself, instead of depending on and trusting God? Does your heart belong to God?

Too often we let emotion and circumstances determine our treasure. We define treasure as something precious, yet it too often is something temporary and self-serving. Too often our time is spent on the here and now, our comfort, our pride, and our own image. Consider the fact that we are God's treasure. He was willing to sacrifice, forgive, and humble Himself for us. His is a heart of purity and love, always focused on close relationships with Him. His treasure is eternal. His heart is love.

Does our heart look the same, or have we claimed the wrong treasure? Is the most important thing in our lives our relationship with God? We let so many things steal our dependence on Him. Our reasoning and motivations erode when we choose the wrong treasure. We allow our passion for God to become secondary in a world that demands its own attention.

God is our treasure. In Him is fulfillment. In Him is true peace. In Him is eternal relationship. Examine your priorities and see what they reveal. Examine the purity of your treasure and see if you are focused on the eternal rather than temporary. Just as we are God's treasure, so is God ours.

"In the house of the upright there is no lack of treasure,
the earnings of the wicked are fraught with anxiety."

PROVERBS 15:6

BE HAPPY

"Be happy at all times, praying constantly. And for all things giving thanks to God for this is what God expects you to do in Christ Jesus."

1 THESSALONIANS 5:16-18

Be happy at all times. It sounds so easy, yet it is so hard to do. This passage does not say to be happy when things go well, or be happy when good things happen to you. We are to be happy at all times. Be happy when things go well, as well as when things go bad. Remember all things work for the good of God. Trust the Lord in all circumstances. Rejoice and be happy knowing that God's promises are true. We can always be happy if and only if we are praying constantly. When we are in consistent prayer God is at the center of our being.

How dare we not be happy? God has given us every reason for true, Christian happiness. He takes on our anxieties and He has paid the price for our sin. God expects us to live in peace and joy for the sake of the amazing gifts and sacrifices of Jesus Christ. A happy Christian can do so much to further the kingdom of God. Let your happiness reveal itself in all the circumstances brought before you. Inner happiness is a gift to you as a Christian.

Ask yourself this question. Are you happy in the Lord? If so, can anybody tell by the way you present yourself? Today think and give praise to God for the blessings He has given you. Then live like a thankful being. You dishonor His gifts by not living in joy. Live thankfully, as though you are blessed with gifts beyond our understanding. Be happy.

"Glad heart means happy face,
where the heart is sad the spirit is broken."

PROVERBS 15:13

PSALM 37

Verses 3-6

"Trust in God and do what is good,
Make your home in the land and live in peace;
Make God your only joy
And He will give you what your heart desires.
Commit your fate to God,
Trust in Him and He will act:
Making your virtue clear as the light,
Your integrity as bright as noon."

MY PERSPECTIVES

HELP OTHERS

"And we urge you, brothers, warn those who are idle, encourage the tired, help the weak, be patient with everyone."

1 THESSALONIANS 5:14

Are you an enabler to the kingdom of God, or are you a stumbling block? Your behavior can do much to further the kingdom of God, or it can turn others away. This verse tells us to be active enablers. We are to provide advice, encouragement, and help to all those around us. Is your life one of patience with others? Do you reflect the grace of God in your dealings with others?

We have been put in a position to enable others and we have to be sure that our actions bring others closer to God. Today, as you deal with other people, be sure you are an enabler. Make it easy for others to see the glory and grace of God, then let His power make them children of God. We are surrounded by people who need our help, encouragement, and patience. Do not give up on anyone, but look for every chance to help. Your words and actions can reveal much about being a Christian. Be concerned about others and live your life finding ways to enable others to come to Christ.

Think how patient God has been with you and thank Him daily for it. With this in mind, show the same patience with others, and strive only to build them up so that they will be able to come to Christ. As a Christian you are to put others before yourself. How much kindness and patience can you show others today? How can you help those less fortunate than yourself? Who can you encourage today? Live your faith today.

"Man's spirit is the lamp of God,
searching his deepest self."

PROVERBS 20:27

REAL EQUALITY

"Then Peter addressed them: 'The truth I have now come to realize,' he said, 'that God does not have favorites, but that anybody of any nationality who fears God and does what is right is acceptable to Him.'"

ACTS 10:34-35

Faith is the great equalizer. Faith brings all believers to a place of equality in the eyes of God. Faith in God brings us into a spirit of unity where everyone is given the same grace. Real equality begins with God.

The truth—all believers can be put into the same basket of truth. We are all sinners, and we are all saved through faith. We are all loved because God is love. These were truths that Peter found to be absolute. In today's world, too many of us want to qualify our truth. We think that truth is dependent on our point of view and our experiences. God is absolute truth. Jesus does not talk about race or gender; He talks about believers. Jesus does not divide, He joins us together with Him. Peter spent years with Jesus, and saw time after time that what Jesus spoke was absolute truth. His truth had authority and power. Jesus was always consistent, unwavering, and assured that He spoke for the Father and always in truth. Jesus could be trusted, and Peter knew that what Jesus taught was always absolute truth. We can depend on Jesus.

Peter had learned a valuable lesson: there are no favorites in the Kingdom of Heaven. Salvation was not reserved for a special few, but it was intended for every living person. Jesus came to save the world, not a race or religion. He loved everyone equally, despite the cultural divisiveness that was all around Him. Peter knew that the Good News was intended for all people and no religion could hold them above any other. Peter knew that mere knowledge and position did not change the amount of love that God has for each of us. We are all equal in the eyes of God. When it comes to the love of God, He plays no favorites. We are acceptable to God through faith just as we are.

Fear God, and have a spirit of unity. Anyone who calls on the name of Jesus will be saved. This is His promise. This is His absolute truth. When we identify and give ourselves to Him, we find humbleness in our actions and compassion for our fellow man. We focus on unity instead of division, and love instead of hate. We see all people as creations of God, uniquely gifted and equally blessed. Fearing God changes everything. Fearing God brings out the best in us and looks for the best in others. Fearing God is a journey of yearning for Him with a goal of being more like Him every day. Fearing God sees past our differences and sees the unity we find with a wide variety of believers, committed to a life focused and prioritized on God instead of ourselves. Fearing God is the way of truth.

We can find our unity with all believers because we know that it is through the same grace of God that we are all saved together. We know that we do not need to elevate ourselves at all costs because God sees heart instead of accomplishment, desire instead of greed, and commitment instead of ego. His gift is for each of us. His love is for us all. His grace is sufficient for everyone. We have a God that wants a relationship with us and has made it possible to be intimate with Him. He loves because that is what He is. It is up to us to do the same. Always do the right thing, regardless of what lies before you. Whoever you can help in front of you, help. Wherever you can show the love of Christ, do it. We are all one in Christ, equal in His eyes.

"Better an equable man than a hero,
A man master of himself than one who takes a city."

PROVERBS 16:32

ARE YOU A SERVANT OF GOD?

"We prove we are God's servants by our purity, knowledge, patience and kindness; by a spirit of holiness, by a love free from affectation; by the word of truth and by the power of God..."

2 CORINTHIANS 6:6

Our life is an open book, displaying our commitments and priorities. We have the opportunity to display our commitment to a life in Christ every day, in every situation. Our actions show the level of our dependence on God, our reliance on His power, and our humility acknowledging His holiness. Challenge after challenge in our daily lives test us continually.

Are the hallmarks of your character based on purity and patience? Do your conversations revolve around your knowledge of God and His truth? Is yours a life of kindness that demonstrates that you rely on the power of God?

We are called to action by this verse and are challenged to not just know the truth, but to live it. We, as servants of God, are called to put our faith into action and to display our commitment to God in all situations. We witness through our actions and our lack of action. Those around you can see the glory of God if we are willing to be obedient to, and alive in, Christ. Our attitude toward the world around us and our efforts to remain faithful to the Spirit of God solidifies our faith.

Does the description of how we prove we are God's servants describe you? What gets in the way of this type of commitment? The proof rests in our attitudes and actions. It is not enough to commit half-heartedly or only when it is easy and convenient. We prove ourselves during both good and bad times, in good and bad situations, in times of plenty and of want.

The Word of Truth and the power of God promise to see us through every situation. Our self-imposed expectations of what we think we deserve by the standards of this world pale in comparison to turning yourself over to God to be His child. We are called to be His light in this world, filled with kindness, purity, and holiness. Our lives should be transparent, letting all our actions be used as a witness to the loving nature of God. It takes obedience, humility, and reliance in God to find true peace. What we prove by these actions are God's love, truth, and spirit. Consider what your life proves. To whom do you belong? Live the life of a child of God!

"He who seduces honest men to evil ways will fall into his own pit. Blameless men are the heirs to happiness."

PROVERBS 28:10

HE IS AT YOUR DOOR

"Look, I am standing at the door, knocking. If one of you hears Me calling and opens the door, I will come in to share his meal, side by side with him."

REVELATION 3:20

Do you ever feel like God is far away? He is right outside your door, waiting to be next to you. Do you ever feel alone? He stands outside your door waiting for you to open it. Do you ever feel that God couldn't love you? He is waiting to sit side-by-side with you. We spend so much effort and time searching for God instead of acknowledging that He is right at our door. He is not going anywhere. He has and always will be within our reach, within our invitation, and within our open heart. Invite Him in.

He is always knocking. The question that we all have to ask ourselves is, what in our lives is causing us not to hear His knocking? What distractions or priorities keep us from being aware of the presence of God? He isn't running past your door. He is just outside. He doesn't kick your door in. He is knocking. He doesn't leave when the knock goes unanswered. He waits patiently. He allows us free will to be the one to open the door. He calls out to each of us individually and waits for the door to be opened. Invite Him in.

His knock and call come with a promise. He promises He will come in and meet you personally and intimately. He wants to be side-by-side with you. He does not want to be God from a distance; He wants to be a part of us and our experiences. He wants a relationship. He wants communication. He wants to share His love. We can share in His power, grace, and mercy when we answer His knock. We can find rest and comfort with Him when we hear and respond to His call. We can rely on His strength, power, and majesty to see us through anything. Invite Him in.

For many of us, it is easy to crack the door open, but only as wide as we think we need. In doing so, we miss the fullness and depth of a personal relationship with God. Throw open the door! Wide open! Invite God in with an openness and honesty that reveals your full self to Him. Let Him reside with you, next to you, and inside of you. Let your ears hear His knock and your eyes see Him fully. Let all of Him inside and let Him dwell with you always. It is an invitation that will change your life for eternity.

"Ears that hears, eye that sees,
God has made both of these."

PROVERBS 20:12

BRING ALL THINGS BEFORE GOD!

"Is any one of you in trouble? He should pray. Is anyone happy? Let him sing songs of praise."

JAMES 5:13

Is God at your center? In both cases in this verse we can see that God should be our focal point. If you are in trouble, bring your problems and anxieties before God in prayer. Take yourself out of the center of the problem and turn it over to God for resolution and peace. If you are happy, you need to sing songs of praise, confirming that all gifts come from God. We are not at the center of our good fortune and happiness, God is. Both cases require us to be humble and recognize that in good times and bad times we must be centered in Christ. This thought leads us to the fact that to stay centered in Christ, we need daily corrections and encouragement.

Whether good or bad, we need constant communication with God, acknowledging that He is our foundation. The recognition of our happiness needs to be praised just as much as our troubles need answers. What takes up the bulk of your conversations with God: the answers to your problems or the acknowledgment of His authority? Do you truly trust God enough to turn your troubles over to Him?

Today, look at your situation and see the many things you have for which you can sing praises. This verse does not say to give a quick thank you, and then move on. It says for all your happiness to sing songs of praise. Glorify God for all His blessings! When you start to count your gifts, you will be surprised how many there are.

Put your problems in perspective. God's gifts are greater than your problems. With God in your center you have the promises of God as your foundation. God will listen to us and give us peace when we bring Him our concerns

"More than all else, keep watch over your heart,
since here are the wellsprings of life."

PROVERBS 4:23

YOU HAVE IT IN YOU

"You will have in you the strength, based on his own glorious power, never to give in, but to bear anything joyfully…".

COLOSSIANS 1:11

The strength is already in you. It is strength greater than your own. It is His glorious power. The joy is already in you. It is a joy greater than your own. It is His joy. The perseverance is already in you. It is perseverance greater than your own. It is His perseverance. We may be weak, but He is strong.

What great confidence this gives us! Too often we look at our weaknesses and feel defeated before we even start the battle. We may feel inadequate and fearful. We may feel powerless. Thank God that He is greater than any problem that stands before us. And the good news is, His power is already in us, ready to be tapped and put into action. The promise of this verse doesn't depend on us, it depends on the glorious power of God. It is a power that allows us to never give in and be joyful in every, every circumstance. It is so easy to be overwhelmed by adversity, feeling out of control and powerless to overcome. Yet God is with us and in us, available to see us through any situation. Even more, He allows us to not only get through any situation, but to do it joyfully! How can this be true? Without God it is not possible, but with God everything is real. The strength is based on the omnipotent God who loves us unconditionally, continually, and fully. He does not leave us when things seem to be too much for us to handle alone. The strength to not only survive, but thrive, is already in us through faith.

It is often very easy to want to give up. Giving in to the negative things around us feels natural sometimes. Without God, life can be very lonely. Thankfully, Christ is not someone who lives externally from us. He is not an entity that is out there somewhere that we have to hunt down in order to have a relationship. He is with us. He is in us. He is for us.

There is nothing greater than God. In Him is the freedom to trust that we have the greatest power imaginable residing inside us, available at all times. God never fails. His strength working in us can see us through any situation.

And what is the price for this power? Faith. We can't work for more power, but we can be sure we have an attitude of joy. It is a joy that goes beyond happiness, based on the knowledge that God is always there with us. He will comfort us in our sorrow and embrace us in our loneliness. We can celebrate in any circumstance that the God of all is on our side and will never fail. We are free because of His power, a power that is already in us.

"Fear of God gives good grounds for confidence,
In Him His children find refuge."

PROVERBS 14: 26

PSALM 37

Verses 23-24

Verses 39-40

"God guides a man's steps,
They are sure, and he takes pleasure in his progress;
He may fall, but never fatally,
Since God supports him by the hand."
"The salvation of the virtuous comes from God,
He is their shelter when trouble comes;
God helps and rescues them,
He saves them because they take shelter in Him."

MY PERSPECTIVES

BE IN TOUCH

"Rejoice with those who rejoice and be sad with those who sorrow."

ROMANS 12:15

God did not create us to be isolated in the world. This verse clearly tells us that we are to be interested in others at a very personal level. We are to be empathetic and have emotional ties with those around us. Rejoicing and sadness are both about emotion. One of our very important functions in life is to support those whose lives we come into contact with, and be there for them in both times of sorrow and rejoicing. This requires that we take the initiative and quit putting ourselves at the center of our universe. This also requires that we connect and make the feelings of other people an important part of our decision making, attitude, and actions. We need to be more outward-looking, searching for ways to connect with others instead of concentrating so much on ourselves.

Be there for the celebrations. Share in the joy of others and find ways to help others rejoice. One thing we never do enough of is to find happiness in the happiness of others. Help them see their gifts and encourage them to focus on the good things that God has provided for us all. Celebrate with them and build up their happiness. We must avoid jealousy and be truly happy for others and their gifts.

In times of sadness, relationships are crucial. Our ability to share sorrow and relieve the burden from others is a gift that needs to be used. The listening ear and comforting hand is ours to give to those in need. Let God use you to soothe wounds and rebuild harmed spirits. In short, make yourself available to others, being an instrument of God in troubled times in the life of others. Show compassion and forgiveness.

Express your joy whenever possible. Be there to build others up and revel in their gifts. God has made us relationship-oriented. Look around you today for chances to smile and rejoice. They are all around you! Display the joy of being a Christian with others and build up the joy. Be a true disciple of God and make yourself available to build up others at every opportunity.

"A kindly glance gives joy to the heart
good news lends strength to the bones."

PROVERBS 15:30

WHY TEST GOD?

"Jesus said to him, 'Scripture also says: You must not put the Lord your God to the test.'"

MATTHEW 4:7

Perhaps you have caught yourself saying some of these things:

Why does God allow...?
Why doesn't God...?
If only God would...
Where is God...?
How could God...?
I would believe if God would just...

Why do we think that we need to make God prove Himself to come into line with our own expectations? Why do we require God to act in a certain way, on our terms? Why do we put God on our timetable, expecting results on our schedule in a way that we deem sufficient? Why do we treat God as an ATM machine, expecting to be able to withdraw His power when we want it and in the amount we think we require? Why do we struggle so mightily letting God be God?

God proves Himself daily. He always provides. He saves us. He loves us. We can trust God because He is God, not because He has to prove something to us. We rely on God because He is God, and He has provided us with righteousness through Christ that we could never obtain on our own. We find rest and peace in God because He is God, and He has won victory for us over sin and death. We can love abundantly because God is love, and He first loved us.

We can eagerly put our trust in God because He is above all and in all. His timing never fails. His power and majesty are shown throughout creation. His plan for all believers is perfect. He is eternal and He is love. Put your doubts aside, and let God be God, the ruler of your heart.

"Trust wholeheartedly in God,
Put no faith in your own perception."

PROVERBS 3:5

FREE YOUR MIND

"Free your minds, then, of encumbrances; control them, and put your trust in nothing but the grace that will be given you when Jesus Christ is revealed."

1 PETER 1:13

Our daily life is bombarded with ideas, wants, and images from the world around us, each striving to take our concentration and focus. Is your mind truly free? The demands and responsibilities of life that seem important at the time can so easily get in the way of reliance on the grace of God. Our minds are a battleground where the ideas of the world seek acceptance and importance.

We have a faulty idea of our own self-importance and feel we can think our way to salvation. Free your mind of the things that get in the way of receiving God's grace. Stop. Prioritize. Receive.

This verse tells us much about human nature. Why do so many things get in the way of clear thinking? Why do we continue to put our trust in ourselves rather than God? We want to give ourselves the place of honor instead of practicing humility before the Giver of Grace.

A free mind is at peace. A free mind accepts. A free mind trusts. Can you control the encumbrances of your mind? Do you filter the bombardment so that nothing gets in the way of your dependence on God? A free mind opens the door for grace, acknowledging that we are not to put our trust in the world around us, our material accumulations, or ourselves.

The only trust that will stand forever is the grace which awaits us that is promised to be revealed. Christ has done the work for us. He has fulfilled the law for us and has paid our ransom. Grace is ours! Don't let your mind be so restricted that you miss what is really important. You cannot worry or think your way to salvation. Keep your mind open and available to God. True peace is His gift.

"The virtuous conduct sets honest men free,
Treacherous men are imprisoned by their own desires."

PROVERBS 11:5

TAKE A TEST

"Examine yourselves to see whether you are in faith; test yourselves."

2 CORINTHIANS 13:5

Can we really pass the test? When we look deep within ourselves, can we say without hesitation that we are in faith? Notice that this passage does not ask if we have faith. It asks if we are in faith. This distinction is quite important. To have faith does not necessarily mean that you continually practice it. You may keep it in reserve to call upon when you think you need it. But to be in faith means that your life and actions are a result of your commitment to your faith. You don't have to think about your faith, it surrounds and dwells within you all the time.

If we are in faith, it will not be hard to answer this question. You will be living every aspect of your life with Christ as the center. You will exude happiness, trust, humility, and confidence. You will be aware of circumstances around you as opportunities to witness your faith. You will not be anxious, and your focus will be to help others and bring them to Christ.

How evident is your faith? So often we keep it hidden, bringing it out only when we think it is necessary. Being in faith allows you to wear your faith on the outside as well as the inside. For all of us who have faith, why don't we focus on not just keeping our faith in our heart, but surrounding ourselves with faith. Be consumed by the power of faith. Let us allow our faith to be displayed, and set ourselves apart as a recognizable Christian, living in faith. May we mature from being individuals with faith to being visible Christians living in faith. Take the test and see the areas of your life that you still want to control. Recognize how often your faith is not part of your actions. Then turn to God, and give Him your life and truly live in faith.

"The fear of God is a life-giving spring,
for eluding the snares of death."

PROVERBS 14:27

YOUR SITUATION

"Brothers, each man, as responsible to God, should remain in the situation God called him to do."

1 CORINTHIANS 7:24

Wherever you are, whatever your situation, you have been placed there by God. How much of your energy is spent looking for opportunities to serve God in your present circumstance rather than trying to get ahead and change your situation?

We are not all blessed with the same blessings, either spiritual or physical. The one thing we can be sure of is that the circumstance you are in is given to you for a purpose, God's purpose. He needs you right where you are, in daily service to Him. Search your heart and your environment for opportunities that God has put before you. We need to fulfill each of our calls by God. In your home, at your job, or with your acquaintances you are responsible to God and His calling for you. Can all those around you tell by your actions that you are in a condition of faithful contentment, or do they see someone trying to change their situation outside of the will of God? We have been given all our gifts, and it is our responsibility to be content in our situation and listen to the call of God.

Put God first today, and praise Him for the opportunities surrounding you. Take a few moments today to consider how you live your daily life. Be sure that you are sensitive to the opportunities you have to witness every day.

"Know your flock's condition well,
take good care of your herds."

PROVERBS 27:23

FILL YOUR MIND

"Finally, brothers, fill your minds with everything that is true, everything that is noble, everything that is good and pure, everything that we love and honor, and everything that can be thought virtuous or worthy of praise."

PHILIPPIANS 4:8

We get to decide what goes into our minds. We can choose to disregard and dispose of everything that is contrary to God, and instead choose to hold firmly to a godly attitude. What we choose to let into our minds can either build us up or tear us down. As we get bombarded day after day, moment by moment, with negative and worldly images and pressures we must always keep our priorities and values on what God intends for us. God's values are the source of peace and contentment, compassion and care, and grace and love. The world's values are a source of competitiveness, comparison, and self-value. Which voice will you let fill your mind?

When I check out the news for the day, the competition for my mind is deafening. Do not let the values of the world into your mind! Paul encourages in this verse to FILL your minds with truth, not leaving any room for falsehood and gossip. We are to FILL our minds with what is honorable, always trying to put the best construction on every situation. We are to FILL our minds with what is good and lovely, celebrating the best in every situation and every person. We are to FILL our minds with thanksgiving to our God who lets us live a life of freedom in His care and grace. Be filled to the brim with love...God's love...and rest in Him. Listen to the voice that fills your mind with the best God has to offer.

There is an abundance of sin and evil in the world. It is competing for real estate in your mind. There is also a God who is greater than any sin and more powerful than any evil, and that God calls you His son or daughter. God loves in abundance. Allow His Spirit to fill your mind to overflowing, refusing to let anything contrary to the love of God find any space. Push the evil out, and replace it with the virtues of God. Refuse to give up any space to anything not worthy of His love. Fill up your mind with the best: God.

"To be afraid of men is a snare,
He who puts his trust in God is secure."

PROVERBS 29:25

PSALM 62

Verses 5-8

"Rest in God alone, my soul!
He is the source of my hope;
With Him alone for my rock, my safety,
My fortress, I can never fall;
Rest in God, my safety, my glory,
The rock of my strength.
In God, I find shelter; rely on Him,
People, at all times;
Unburden your hearts to Him,
God is a shelter for us."

MY PERSPECTIVES

PROCLAIM

"And He said to them, 'Go out to the whole world; proclaim the Good News to all creation.'"

MARK 16:15

How does your life proclaim the Good News of salvation given by grace through faith in Jesus Christ? Does your approach toward a life of gratitude and honor of Christ meet this directive by Christ?

Dictionary.com defines the word proclaim as:
to announce or declare in an official or formal manner
to announce or declare in an open or ostentatious way
to indicate or make known publicly or openly
to extol or praise publicly: i.e. Let them proclaim the Lord

When we proclaim Christ, we proclaim the absolute truth. Through Christ, we are saved and through Christ, we are included in His plan of salvation. He is the means by which we are saved.

A life devoted to proclaiming the Good News is a life lived in freedom, a visible and obvious dedication to Him. When we live out our proclamation of faith, we are distinct from the rest of the world as we put our trust and hope in Christ only. Our life can be a continual declaration that we rely on His grace, His promises, and His power to lead us to eternity. Live a life of proclamation that shows the world we can live abundantly and lovingly when Christ is our Savior.

At a time when the world is trying to push God further away, we are told by Christ to let this world see our faith, proudly and openly declaring our trust in God. Be bold. Be open. Never shy away from letting the world see your reliance on our loving God. The Good News is intended for us as individuals and for the entire world of His creation. We know the Good News. We experience His love. Take every opportunity to share that relationship with Christ to everyone. Proclaim Christ with a life devoted to Him and with words that speak with love and compassion. We are victorious in Him.

"My mouth proclaims the truth,
wickedness is hateful to my lips."

PROVERBS 8:7

IMITATE WHAT IS GOOD

"Dear friend, do not imitate what is evil but what is good. Anyone who does what is good is from God. Anyone who does what is evil has not seen God."

3 JOHN 11

How easy it is to imitate evil. We are surrounded by evil every day and it is so easy to go along with the ways of the world. The demands of our everyday life have us focusing on worldly ways. How do you change your focus? What courage and strength it takes to imitate good!

Do you look for the good in every situation and strive to magnify it, or do you merely accept the evil around you and thereby make a place for it in your life? Our complacency serves to strengthen evil. This passage tells us that the evildoers have not seen God.

Do they continue to do evil perhaps because they do not see God in you? How do you expect there to be change if we do not become an active participant in the revelation of God to them? We are instructed to actively imitate what is good, removing evil imitations from our lives. This is not an easy process in our world. It takes courage to break the patterns of evil, courage to be willing to go in a different direction, and courage to openly reveal our priorities to those who have not seen God. It is up to us to imitate good and let the power of God open the eyes of those who have not seen Him. When we do good we are told we are from God. What an awesome honor and what an awesome responsibility.

Let us pray for the courage to do good so that we can let those who have not seen God know that God is actively working in us. Let us pray for strength to recognize the evil in this world and not imitate it. Let your imitations be those of Christ. Think about your actions today. Be sure that you are imitating good at every opportunity. May God help all of us to live and act like followers of Christ.

"He walks secure whose ways are honorable,
but he who follows crooked ways is soon discovered."

PROVERBS 10:9

BE PREPARED FOR AN ATTACK

"You are well aware, then, that anybody who tries to live in devotion to Christ is certain to be attacked; while these wicked impostors will go from bad to worse, deceiving others and deceived themselves."

2 TIMOTHY 3:12-13

Do not be surprised when you are persecuted! Being a child of God does not shield you from hardships. Here we are told that it will only get worse as time goes on. Do not be surprised! We are not called to be in a perfect world, but to live a Christian life in a world full of sin.

Perseverance and dedication to live a godly life in the face of an ever-worsening sinful world is something to pray about. Pray for the strength and wisdom to see things for what they are and not be deceived by the worsening deceivers. They will be persistent and committed in their perception, even fooling themselves. Keep your eyes open and be aware. Let the persecutions you face serve to strengthen your faith, knowing God will provide the strength and direction to face the deceptions.

Since you know you will be persecuted, do not let it separate you from God. Persecution does not come from God, but the strength to overcome it does. Feel secure in the knowledge that the deceivers cannot take away the grace of God! We are blessed, even through the trials we face. God provides us with sufficient strength to not only persevere, but to live in peace and happiness, despite our external circumstances. Do not let outside influences affect the spirit within you.

Look closely at your trials today, be aware to not be deceived, and know that God is always there to see you through.

"Do not be envious of wicked men
or wish for their company,
for their hearts are scheming violence,
their lips talking of mischief."

PROVERBS 24:1-2

YOUR FULFILLMENT

"In His body lives the fullness of divinity, and in Him you too find your own fulfillment, in the one who is the head of every Sovereignty and Power."

COLOSSIANS 2:9-10

Have you ever searched for meaning and purpose in your life? Look to Jesus. Have you ever felt empty or useless? Look to Jesus. Have you ever felt like something is missing? Look to Jesus.

In His body lives the fullness of divinity. Jesus was real flesh and blood and was every bit the fullness of God. Jesus was the complete, full embodiment of the Almighty God. He was not just a messenger of good things, a prophet, or a speaker of truth. The Father did not use Jesus as a mirror or endow Him with some special gifts. He was the fullness of God, in every way, total divinity and total sovereign God. When we choose to follow Jesus, we are following the fullness of God.

In Him, you too can find your own fulfillment. As a person of faith, you have a wonderful purpose ahead of you. You are free to follow Christ, love like Christ, and live like Christ. The trials and cares of the world cannot take away the true divinity of Christ, nor diminish your attitude and commitment. Living a life saturated by the Holy Spirit is a commitment to setting your goals at the highest mark by doing the will of our Creator, Lord, and Savior. There is no need to feel half-full when our faith in Christ can fill us to more than the top. His fullness gives us a richness of experience that goes beyond our expectations. Being filled with His love gives us the freedom to love unconditionally and passionately. His fullness lets us be compassionate and generous, patient and forgiving. In Him we are truly fulfilled as individuals.

He is the head of every Sovereignty and Power. There is no need to concern ourselves with the problems of the worldview when we hold dearly to the view of Christ. We can be renewed and refreshed with the knowledge that the person in whom we trust is all-powerful and full of grace. Whenever evil seems to triumph, we need to remind ourselves that God reigns supreme. He will prevail. He is justice and love. He is peace and grace. He is the most powerful, most fulfilling, and most forgiving entity. We can rest in Him because He is the final authority and wields all the power. Our faith, trust, and dedication to Him are the best purposes we can ever have. In Him, we are reconciled and able to have a relationship with the Almighty God. How blessed we are.

"God made everything for its own purpose,
Yes, even the wicked for the day of disaster."

PROVERBS 16:4

LONG BEFORE DAWN

"In the morning, long before dawn, He got up and left the house and went off to a lonely place and prayed there."

MARK 1:35

Long before dawn, before the demands on Jesus were present, He went to be alone with God. Far away from the distractions and the hurry, Jesus went to be alone with God. Setting Himself apart from the everyday grind of life, Jesus went to be alone with God. In the midst of a world that wants to catch you up into the middle of life, where do you get alone with God?

The competition for our attention every day is exhaustive and never-ending. We get wrapped up in "important" things of life, and push meaningful things aside. We let whatever is right in front of us steal our soul, while God patiently waits. When was the last time you stopped and listened?

Jesus had power and authority. He had right and priority. Yet He prayed. Jesus had all knowledge and all presence. Yet He prayed. Jesus had all wisdom and all honor. Yet He prayed.

Life can be such a whirlwind of activity and concern, yet we too often forget the importance of being in full communion with God in the gift of silence. When do we not just hear but listen? When do we not just act, but respond? When do we not ask God to answer our prayers, but ask how we can be the answer to someone else's prayer? How can we let aloneness with God lead to growth and obedience?

There are many instances in the life of Jesus that He went to be alone purposefully to pray with God alone. No motives. No demands. Just intimacy. Just identity. Just love.

In the midst of life on the go, train yourself to slow down. In times when life demands you, remember God wants you. In times of discouragement, remember God loves you. In times of stress, remember God comforts you. Quiet time with God is a gift that gives and gives and gives. Listening to God is a gift that gives and gives and gives. When you feel empty, God fills to overflowing. Be still and know that He is God.

"Many are the plans of the human heart,
But the purpose of God-that stands firm."

PROVERBS 19:21

LOOK UPWARD

"Since you have been brought back to true life with Christ, you must look for the things that are in heaven, where Christ is, sitting at God's right hand."

COLOSSIANS 3:1

Need advice to overcome a problem or concern? Look up to Christ.
Need direction in your life? Look up to Christ.
Trying to form an opinion on something? Look up to Christ.
Trying to find purpose and meaning? Look up to Christ.
Wondering where hope and joy is? Look up to Christ.
Struggling with guilt and doubt? Look up to Christ.
Stress and anxiety overtaking you? Look up to Christ.
Feeling alone or unworthy? Look up to Christ.
Searching for forgiveness? Look up to Christ.
Needing rest and peace? Look up to Christ.
Realize you need to be thankful? Look up to Christ.

You get the idea. If we really believe that Christ has saved us, then we must find joy in that victory and share His love. He is our source, foundation, and strength in all we do. We are so fortunate to have a God that truly cares for each of us, understands all our hardships, and has shown His mercy and love to all of us through Christ. Christ did His work here on earth and now sits at the right hand of the Father in victory, letting each of us share in that satisfaction. With Christ, disappointment in ourselves turns into achievement and victory. With Christ, we do not need to grade ourselves on earthly values because we have the eternal assurance of a merciful God. With Christ, the conflict and disunity of this world has no effect on our relationship with God.

Be who you are, a saved child of God. We have so many things that try to distract us from the absolute truth of the love of God. Live as you are, a saved child of God. A world that is trying so hard to push God away cannot change our reliance and faith in Him. Nothing can separate us from the love of God when we put faith first. Choose joy. God loves you.

Want to give praise and honor? Look up to Christ and be what you are: a saved child of God.

"This was what he used to teach me,
'Let your heart treasure what I have to say,
keep my principles and you shall live.'"

PROVERBS 4:4

PSALM 116

Verses 1-2

Verses 4-6

"Alleluia!
I love!
For God listens to my entreaty;
He bends down to listen to me when I call."
"God, rescue me!
God is righteous and merciful
Our God is tenderhearted;
God defends the simple,
He saved me when I was brought to my knees."

MY PERSPECTIVES

ALL THINGS WORK FOR GOOD

"And we know that all things work together for good to those who love God."

ROMANS 8:28

What great comfort this verse gives! We can be assured that God's plan for us is ongoing and real. We do not have to worry about circumstances, but only have to be sure that our love for God stays alive within us and we never lose faith.

Perseverance through circumstances keeps us part of the good that God has planned for us. We need discipline. Hardships strengthen our faith, foster our growth, and allow us to mature. The trust that all things work together for good allows us to stop looking at isolated circumstances and to realize that God has long-range plans for us. Obviously it is not our nature to be so far-sighted. We have conditioned ourselves to react circumstance by circumstance without trust. We allow circumstances to dictate our actions and determine our attitude.

The assurance in this verse comes in the second part, "for those who love God." Our focus has to be on God, not our circumstances. Our challenge is to trust God in all circumstances, both good and bad. This allows us the freedom to live in peace and joy, even when we are challenged. Can you look past what you consider a hardship today and trust that your challenge is working for good? Can you place your focus on God today and praise Him for the challenges placed before you? Can you reflect God's love to others in every circumstance you face?

If we can faithfully trust God, His promise is real. Allow yourself to be part of God's plan for you today. Let your love of God control your actions and live with confidence in every situation.

"The wicked man flees when no one is after him,
the virtuous man is bold as a lion."

PROVERBS 28:1

DO NOT BE TIMID

"God's gift was not a spirit of timidity, but the Spirit of power, and love, and self-control."

2 TIMOTHY 1:7

God's gift is power! God's gift is love! God's gift is self-control! Too often Christians display God's gifts in such a way that they shrink from the declaration that God is power! Too often Christians feel that patience, understanding, and servanthood are signs of weakness.

We fear confrontation and make our spirituality private and tucked away, fearing ridicule if we openly display our faith and trust in God. That type of living is not the way that God intended when He gave us the gift of His Spirit. We are the recipients of more power than we could ever realize when we live filled with His Spirit. Everyday actions and decisions influenced by God's power can change lives and attitudes.

We are not the source of the power, but when we live with His Spirit in us, we are God's tool, used to be His conduit for His purpose to influence the world around us. God's gift of the Spirit of love changes relationships and outlooks like nothing else. Compassion and empathy open the hearts of both the giver and receiver of God's love. God is a God of relationship that thrives on love.

So many times we think of self-control as missing out on the fun times or depriving ourselves of what we think we want. Self-control is the best indicator of where we put our trust. Living for yourself and desiring what you want, when you want it, takes God out of the equation. Self-control highlights that God knows best for us. Obedience to His Word shows our respect and reliance on Him.

Do you live your life with the full power of God or do you avoid uncomfortable situations? We are called to be bold in our faith, using every situation God puts before us to be vehicles for God's power and promises to be unveiled. Be bold! Let His power fill you! Allow God's power within you to shout to the world through your words and actions that you are His.

"An open town, and without defenses,
Such is the man lacking self-control."

PROVERBS 25:28

WORK

"My greetings to Prisa and Aquila, my fellow workers in Christ Jesus, who risked death to save my life."

ROMANS 16:3

Work: exertion or effort directed to produce or accomplish something; labor; toil.

Being a follower of Christ Jesus requires effort on our part. Too often we think that our level of faith and our relationship to Christ is a one-way street. We wrongly assume it is up to Him to reach us. We want to be a casual observer, not needing to commit ourselves to action. We do not want to roll up our sleeves and prepare ourselves to go to work for Jesus.

Too often we ask the wrong questions. Why don't I feel inspired? I will wait for God to inspire me. Why don't I feel close to God? Where is He when I need Him? I will wait for Him to come to me. Why is there so much strife in the world? I will let God take care of it. Why do I feel lost? I wonder when God will find me. In other words, we want all the benefits, but too often, do not want to put in the work. He is there for us. Are we there for Him?

This verse is one of several that Paul wrote to remember all those who had committed themselves to work for the cause of Christ. They were in a hostile environment, with an enormous task in front of them as they revealed the Good News, helping create a new community of believers. They were willing to sacrifice, even unto death if necessary, in the name of Christ. They were willing to do the work, to accomplish, to labor, and to toil for Christ. They sacrificed and put themselves at risk, all to the glory of Christ.

All of us need to be committed and consistent in our work for Jesus. There is no room for complacency or indifference. Our work for Jesus is important and a necessary part to bring the Good News of salvation to a world in need. It is an effort that needs to be resilient and unwavering in our attention and actions. It is an effort that needs to persevere and shine in difficulty, hold fast, and be bold at all times. We are working for Christ! Be ready to put in a good life's work.

Our relationship with Jesus needs our attention and commitment. It needs communication and respect, effort and desire. It needs to be important and trustful, prioritized and true. It needs our work. Christ wants our hands involved and our minds engaged as we set out to live a life for Him. Many of us spend a majority of our lives at a job, forgetting that our real work is for Christ. Work for Him at work, play, and at leisure. Set your sights on Him. Do the heavy lifting when required. Our work will always be rewarded.

"Give her a share in what her hands have worked for,
And let her works tell her praises at the city gates."

PROVERBS 31:31

REMAIN FAITHFUL

"You and I are not the sort of people who draw back, and are lost by it; we are the sort who keep faithful until our souls are saved."

HEBREWS 10:39

Once you have received Christ and committed to live in Him, how does your life change in response? Is it the most important thing in your life? Do you count yourself among those who keep faithful to the end, no matter what things try to stand in your way? Do you live boldly for Christ, energized with the knowledge that you are a saved soul through His grace and sacrifice? Do you live with confidence and peace, reliant on your relationship with Christ? Or do you draw back?

Believers in Christ do not draw back. Believers in Christ do not live timidly. Believers in Christ do not live in fear or with apprehension. We are the sort that remains faithful, using His Word as our guide and His promises as our hope. We can live with patience and contentment knowing that God's eternal plan includes each of us. We can live as servants, happily and willingly setting out to do God's work here on earth. Our lives here are not about accumulation, power, or self. It is about service, obedience, sacrifice, and others. Our rewards are eternal in nature and our job is to remain faithful.

No doubt there is a constant battle going on with things trying to pull us away from our faithfulness. The world gets in our way. We too often lack the discipline to say "no" to the temptations that bombard us. We get in our own way to faithfulness as well. We admire wealth, power, and position more than we honor sacrifice and service. Our egos too often take priority over our servant hearts. Our faithfulness takes a back seat to our desire, and soon our faith is not apparent at all. There is an answer. Jesus.

Stand firm against the world's standards and your own failures. Do not be lost by drawing back. Live your faithfulness every moment of every day with excitement and passion. Be determined to keep your faithfulness alive, real, and important. Set your priorities squarely on Him. You will be saved!

"No man is made secure by wickedness,
But nothing shakes the roots of the virtuous man."

PROVERBS 12:3

LET PEACE REIGN

"And may the peace of Christ reign in your hearts,
because it is for this that you were called together as parts of one body.
Always be thankful."

COLOSSIANS 3:15

Peace. One of the hardest lessons we all have to learn is that there is a difference between the peace of the world and the peace of Christ. Too often we equate peace to the absence of conflict. We think of peace as being left alone, finding a quiet spot, and not being challenged. We define peace as the opposite of war and look at it mainly as a personal safety issue, not requiring interaction or relationships that might take us out of our comfort zone. The peace of the world is temporary and always at risk of changing. It is a situation, not a way of life. It can be lost in an instant.

The peace of Christ is a gift we receive when we, through faith, find our hearts in harmony with Him. It is about unity, trust, and respect for the absolute authority and power found only in Him. It is ours despite challenge or circumstance, finding its place in our hearts when He rules it completely. The peace of Christ is not about circumstance, it is about faith in the promises of God. Our heart rests when we live assured and forgiven, involved and alive in Christ. Our heart multiplies that peace with a spirit of thanksgiving, knowing that His peace is always there, never subject to change. His peace is real, lasting, and complete. It is a peace we cannot lose when Christ reigns in our hearts.

It is this peace of Christ that must have full authority and dominance in our hearts. It must reign! This peace of Christ in our hearts is our foundation, standard by which all things are judged, and source for our hope. It brings joy to the believer, in every circumstance. It yields trust in Christ, not ourselves. It gives a peace built on His power, not our own. Only a heart ruled by Christ can find the real peace we all search and long for.

Be thankful. Nothing changes a heart more than the realization that a life focused on thankfulness is a life that mirrors the love of Christ. Gratitude makes way for empathy, concern, and awareness. A thankful heart is a giving heart. A thankful attitude lets love flow freely, abundantly, and selflessly. In order to allow our heart to be reigned by the love of Christ, it needs to be in a thankful disposition. He reigns, and we gain. His deity yields our peace. His love changes us from the inside out. Be thankful.

"More than all else, keep watch over our heart,
Since here are the wellsprings of life."

PROVERBS 4:23

TACT

"Be tactful with those who are not Christians and be sure you make the best use of your time with them."

COLOSSIANS 4:4

The manner in which a Christian talks, acts, and thinks should never be a barrier to witnessing for Christ to a non-believer. There should always be wisdom and compassion when representing yourself as a Christian to the world. There should be patience and humility in all our dealings with non-believers so that they can see the best of Christ in us. Look at some of the synonyms for being tactful:

considerate, sensitive, understanding, thoughtful, delicate, diplomatic, discreet, discerning, judicious, politic, perceptive, subtle, careful

Do these words describe your interactions with those who are not Christians? Society is more interested in demanding attention and shouting the loudest. Judgments are confirmed without evidence and suspicions are bandied about like they are fact. Differences are ridiculed and decried. Sensationalism and provocation are everyday expectations. But in this verse, Paul tells us to be different. God is not served by pompous, arrogant declarations. We are to serve as Christ served. That means we must take up the mantle of humility, obedience, and love.

Too often the perception of a Christian is an intolerant attitude with a sanctimonious mentality. Unfortunately, oftentimes that reputation has been deserved as many of us fail to live up to the direction in this verse. We are too often guilty of projecting mannerisms and actions that do not shed the best light on our Savior and our faith. People hold their views of God and faith very personally and these views need to be treated tactfully. We must never force our views on anyone and surely not change the message of the Good News, but we must display wisdom in our approaches.

Christian witness for most of us will be displayed in the everyday, normal occurrences in our lives. We can witness by demonstrating characteristics and choices that go against the grain of today's society. We can be humble and considerate, unafraid that those traits weaken our faith. We can be diplomatic and perceptive because we know that our foundation on Christ is a strong foothold. We can be understanding and forgiving because God understands our failings and forgives. We can dare to be different in Christ!

A brash and boastful voice can be harmful, no matter how dedicated one might be. A spirit of judgment can separate others from Christ. Let us all be careful and thoughtful, slow to speak and quick to listen, and be willing to show the restraint and confidence that we have through Christ. Remember, Christ is always the focus, reason, and hope. Let us never get in the way through our actions of letting the Holy Spirit work.

"There are some whose thoughtless words pierce like a sword,
But the tongue of the wise brings healing."

PROVERBS 12:18

PSALM 25

Verses 17-18
Verses 20-21

"Relieve the distress of my heart,
Free me from my sufferings.
See my misery and pain,
Forgive all my sins!"
"Watch over my soul, rescue me;
let me not be shamed; I take shelter in You.
Let innocence and integrity be my protection,
Since my hope is in You, God."

MY PERSPECTIVES

WHERE IS YOUR HOMELAND?

"For us, our homeland is in heaven, and from heaven comes the Savior we are waiting for, the Lord Jesus Christ, and He will transfigure these wretched bodies of ours into copies of His glorious body."

PHILIPPIANS 3:20-21

Where is your homeland? Is it here on earth or is it in heaven? Where is your focus? Does the spirit within you come from heaven and will you return there? This verse offers such peace. As believers in Christ, we know where we come from and we also know that Christ promises to take us home with renewed and perfect bodies. Why do we spend so much time focused on earthly things when we know our eventual home is in heaven? Why do we spend so much time here on earth forgetting to focus our eyes upward, knowing that heaven is our true homeland?

So many of our concerns and worries would disappear if we would spend more time on bended knees looking up rather than running in the worldly rat race that grips us so tightly. How wonderful it is to know that all the worries of our bodies will one day be removed, transformed into copies of God Himself. No longer captives of worldly thoughts, desires, and pursuits, we will be with God, in heaven. Our homeland defines us. It gives us our culture, customs, heritage, and references. Those of us who are in Christ have heaven as our homeland. We can claim a culture based on love, faith, sacrifice, humility, and service. We know the attributes that we should be portraying in our daily lives. These attributes are part of us, ingrained into our consciousness through faith. Do you display your heritage as a Christian? Rejoice in the confidence of this verse. For us, our homeland is in heaven. Be sure you live like it! Our reunion with Christ is waiting. Praise God.

"He who despises the word will destroy himself,
he who respects the commandment will be safe."

PROVERBS 13:13

PATIENCE

"Refute falsehood, correct error, call to obedience—but do all with patience and with the intention of teaching."

2 TIMOTHY 4:2

All of us should be on a path to find truth. All of us should not let misinformation go unchecked. All of us should pursue and recognize the value of service and obedience to a God that loves us. All of these virtues need to be shared and expounded, but never in a way that would put up any barrier to others. A real teacher teaches the truth, from a confidence that their lesson is without error or misconception. Jesus was the real teacher of the absolute Truth. He did refute the falsehoods of the day and corrected the errors of men who were putting themselves, rules, and religion ahead of real relationship with God. Jesus was the ultimate example of obedience as He carried out the plan from the Father that would save a sinful world. He also calls us to obedience, living the believing life because of His love and care for each of us.

Jesus did not force His teaching on anyone, but instead taught by example and Word. He was patient with the crowds. They were seeking His miracles and healing, but at the same time doubted His deity. He patiently corrected those that persecuted Him as He showed them the errors of their thinking and living. He saw evil and sin all around, yet patiently taught the Truth at every opportunity. Time after time He taught His disciples valuable lessons, even when they let their egos and misunderstanding get in the way.

Jesus never condoned bad behavior or compromised His teaching. He did not seek position or popularity. He came to serve and to save. He saw legalistic religion missing the importance of relationship and witnessed how the religious leaders of that day put ritual ahead of compassion in their quest to earn position with the Father. He was willing to face the circumstances of His truth and authority, never backing down from living in love, compassion, and obedience.

We are surrounded by a world that is full of error and selfishness. Yet, we are called to live a life of obedience to God. We need to set ourselves apart from the lies, yet not be condescending because we too are sinners. Our real relationship with God is one that should continue to evolve and grow as we strive to learn the lessons and live the life of the Truth. The patience that God shows towards us is the perfect example of how we need to show patience to others.

Jesus was not afraid to speak the Truth in all situations. He revealed the errors of man and testified to the sinfulness of mankind. He was gentle. He taught by His Word. He taught by His example. He let people find the Truth through Him. People saw the Father through Him. We are saved through Him. Are you ever an obstacle to anyone finding that same Truth? Do you share the patience that Jesus showed with all the people who were misguided? Is your heart with Jesus?

In all that we do we should stand for Jesus. Our attitude must be one of patience and teaching as we stand. Let His power do the work as we stand firmly in Him. Be bold. Be strong. Be obedient. Be humble.

"The fear of God is a school of wisdom,
Humility goes before honor."

PROVERBS 15:33

WHAT WORDS REVEAL

"So I tell you this, that for every unfounded word men utter they will answer on Judgment Day, since it is by your words you will be acquitted, and by your words condemned."

MATTHEW 12:36-37

Nothing reveals what is in a man's heart more than the words he speaks. Whatever fills your heart will flow out of your mouth. It does not take long when listening to someone speak to know much about their character. When you speak, what do people see? Do your words reveal ego, self-reliance, and envy or humbleness, charity, and reliance on God?

We will have to answer for our ill-chosen words and untrusting hearts. We can also show through our words that God dwells in our heart. What do your words say about your heart? How many of your words are chosen to comfort, serve, or build up someone else? Do your words display the peace that comes from trusting God instead of yourself and the world? How many words are used for complaining about your own circumstances or perceived earthly injustices?

If God fills your heart, He will be revealed through your words. Our words need to be about peace, not intolerance. Our words need to be used to glorify God, His promises, and His gifts. Our words must be filled with truth. Innuendo, slander, and gossip should stake no claim in the heart or on the tongue of a Christian.

God has given us a great vehicle to witness our faith in Him, our words. Pure words can change lives and strengthen those around us. Pure words are used by the Holy Spirit to work wonders in the hearts of those who hear. God uses us and our words to be His mouthpiece to spread the Good News of Christ's redemptive sacrifice. He uses us and our words to be His comforting presence.

As you go about your day today, listen to the words that you speak. Be aware of negative words that come out of your mouth. Be aware of the effect that your spiritual words have on others and yourself. What you say is revealing your heart. What are your words saying about you?

"The mouth of the fool works his own ruin,
His lips are a snare for his own life."

PROVERBS 18:7

DO NOT BE TRAPPED

"Make sure that no one traps you and deprives you of your freedom by some secondhand, empty, rational philosophy based on the principles of this world instead of on Christ."

COLOSSIANS 2:8

Society offers improvement with lightning speed. There are quick fixes, new and different ideas, and cutting-edge ways to find happiness. We are told how to make things easier, how to look better, how we can relax and find enjoyment. The hard part is so many of these things make rational sense. We can talk ourselves into believing these bombardments without too much effort.

Beware!! Ask yourself how many of these new ideas and principles are founded on the ways of the world instead of Christ. They promise much, but are empty of real freedom. So many new ideas tell us how we can think ourselves into freedom if we trust the power of our personal positive thinking. They tell us to take control of our lives and they put the answers to our problems before us in a neat package.

Beware!! The key to true freedom is to give control of your life to God, not to take charge of it. We need to turn our lives over to Him, depending on His promises. Sometimes the answers to our problems are not supposed to be laid before us in a nice, neat package. There are times when it is God's plan for you to test your faith in order for you to grow. All of the promises of the world try to separate us from listening to God and His promises. Freedom cannot be found in thinking our way out of problems or by rationalizing what we know is wrong. True freedom comes from releasing ourselves to God to live as a child of God, even with its difficulties.

Do not look for the easy way out that the world tries to offer, but instead accept the challenges put before you with happiness, peace, and freedom.

"There is a way that some think right,
but it leads in the end to death."

PROVERBS 14:12

FAN THE FLAME

"That is why I am reminding you now to fan into a flame the gift that God gave you when I laid my hands on you."

2 TIMOTHY 1:6

Intensity. Passion. Total commitment. These things are needed to live a life that is on fire for Christ. If you are like me, it is easy to choose convenient Christianity. I find myself living my life on my terms, turning to God only when necessary. I keep my faith to myself in a desire to be non-confrontational. I have convinced myself that a quiet Christian is a good Christian. But what does Paul say? Fan the flame! Let God's grace light you on fire for Christ. Burn white-hot with an obvious identity with Christ!

Paul's message to Timothy applies so well to each and every Christian. Paul is encouraging Timothy to recognize that with God's gift comes power, the power to ignite an entire way of life and influence those around us. God's gifts are intended to overflow from us to all those with whom we interact. We are to let the heat of His grace for each believer burn brightly and visibly. A life on fire for Christ is a life lived in the fullness of His glory.

We have all seen what happens to hot embers when air is pushed over them. They glow white with intensity. They are set aflame with the wind. They emit heat that wasn't there before. We as Christians are those embers.

Will we let the heat dissipate and go out, or encourage a life in Christ that will ignite us to new heights? May the power through Christ set you on fire!

Think of what God has given you—forgiveness, sanctification, salvation. Why? Because He first loved you. You are an heir with Christ to all the gifts of God. Set yourself on fire to let these gifts shine.

"The light of virtuous men burns bright,
The lamp of the wicked goes out."

PROVERBS 13:9

GOD CANNOT BE MOCKED

"Do not be deceived: God cannot be mocked.
A man reaps what he sows."

GALATIANS 6:7

You cannot be a hypocrite in God's kingdom. Our actions and faith will determine our future. To be a child of God is to be committed physically, emotionally, and spiritually to God. We cannot expect to live in a manner that mocks God only to expect God's blessings. God cannot be mocked. He cannot be fooled. He knows your motives, He knows your mind, and He knows your soul. Actions and words can fool people some of the time, but God knows your heart. There is no ambivalence.

Are you a child of God? Will the decisions you make today sow the seeds of salvation? Will your actions and words reveal the true nature of God's grace? Do not fool yourself! You cannot put off living your faith for another day or figure you will turn to God if some difficulty arises. You cannot negotiate with God.

Take time today to look at your decisions. How have you treated others today? Did your actions build up others or did they serve to build up yourself? Your heart is plain to God. We cannot expect to reap God's glory without sowing His seeds. Be active today being truthful with yourself. Choose carefully the seeds you sow. Make your harvest honest, truthful, and filled with the promises of God.

"Let God be pleased with a man's way of life
and he makes his very enemies into friends."

PROVERBS 16:7

PSALM 86

Verses 3-8

"You are my God, take pity on me, Lord,
I invoke You all day long;
Give Your servant reason to rejoice, for to You, Lord, I lift my soul.
Lord, You are good and forgiving,
Most loving to all who invoke You;
God, hear my prayer, listen to me as I plead.
Lord, in trouble I invoke You,
And You answer my prayer;
There is no god to compare with You,
No achievement to compare with Yours."

MY PERSPECTIVES

DO NOT BE ANGRY

"In your anger do not sin: do not let the sun go down while you are still angry, and do not give the devil a foothold."

EPHESIANS 4:26-27

Nothing good comes out of letting anger have power in your life. What a mighty tool the devil has when our anger leads to sin. Our anger left unresolved gives the devil a place in our heart, eating away at us and changing our perceptions. Anger is a natural emotion, one that is difficult to control. Think how many times you have said something in anger that you wish you could take back.

Think how anger has changed your perspective in a situation. This verse does not say don't get angry. It says do not sin in your anger. It tells you to keep anger in its place. It also tells us to deal with anger within the day. Anger left unresolved multiplies into a force of its own. We are to be right with God, right with others, and right with ourselves each and every day. Dealing with our anger daily allows us to keep things in perspective and look at the larger picture. Otherwise, we give the devil the foothold he so desperately wants to eat away at us from the inside.

Are you angry about anything today? If so, do what needs to be done to recognize it for what it really is? With the help and guidance of God, come to terms with your anger. Be at peace each night. Do not let anger control your actions. Keep the devil away from your heart.

"A quick-tempered man commits rash acts,
The prudent man will be long-suffering."

PROVERBS 14:17

VALUE

"A spiritual man, on the other hand, is able to judge the value of everything, and his own value is not to be judged by other men."

1 CORINTHIANS 2:15

Spiritual things have a completely different basis of value than secular things. One has eternal value, the other is temporary. One focuses on God, the other on self. One finds wholeness in the act of sacrifice, the other defines success in material terms. One leads to peace and joy, the other to anxiousness and pride. What set of values do you use to determine worth? In this age we are inundated by images that try to define value and worth. We are told to display our value and are encouraged to live beyond our means, wanting it all, and wanting it all NOW. We are becoming a society that has little patience, willing to put our futures on credit.

This verse says very plainly that we, as followers of Christ, are different. Our values are not in things, but in relationships. Our joy is not dependent on conditions or circumstances, but instead is based on the peace and promises that come from God. Our value cannot be judged by men because the world's standards do not apply. We find spiritual peace and contentment in a life filled with the Holy Spirit. We are not defined by our power, wealth, or position. Our goals are different. Our reasons are different. Our methods are different. Our disappointments are temporary and our tribulations serve to give us patience and understanding. Look for the potential for good in every situation and depend on faith to give everything value. Ours is an eternal value.

Have you examined your motivations lately? What do you value? What do you base your values on? How do you judge the value of others? It is a constant battle, but one that can change your attitudes dramatically. God has guaranteed your value through the sacrifice of Christ. Beware of using worldly standards to judge the worth of others. That judgment is not ours to make. Our job is to remain spiritual, seeing clearly the worth of all of God's creations and acting in obedience with pure motivations.

"The blessing of God is what brings riches,
To this hard toil has nothing to add."

PROVERBS 10:22

LOVE IN EVERYTHING

"Let everything you do be done in love."

1 CORINTHIANS 16:14

It is always time to love. Wouldn't it be a different world if we made love the dominant feature of our lives? What do you do for a living? Answer: I love unconditionally. How do you put up with the drama in your family? Answer: I love unconditionally. How is work going? Answer: Great. It gives me an opportunity to show love.

When we look around us, we see the effects of pushing love aside. Anger and contradiction are the attitudes of the day. A "me first" focus sets love off to the side to be used when convenient. The failure to love leads to corruption. Politicians argue and lie, businesses take advantage, and governments gather power with ill intentions. Families struggle, churches suffer, and friends bicker when they forget to love. In these times we need to step back and see what we are doing to ourselves through our failure to love, then change. A true, honest look at ourselves and our failure to always love in everything will let us see the results of withholding love. The two keywords in this verse are EVERYTHING and LOVE. If we are to do everything in love it requires a complete commitment to a way of life and development of part of our character. Our focus on love filters our behavior. Our focus on love picks our words. Our focus on love changes our attitude. Being able to love at all times is a gift, a precious gift from God. He loves. He is love. Most importantly, loving at all times is our response to the love of God shown to us. He loves us as we are, despite our weakness, unconditionally. He loves us in our failures and in our triumphs, during our struggles and our joy, and in our depressions and our exhilaration. He loves in everything. With His love as our guide, we are free to love fully and completely. When we love in everything there is no individual motive, but only a heart set on nurturing others. When we love in everything we experience the presence of God in action, being used to extend the love of His grace to everyone.

If we want to be known for anything, let us all be known as a person who loves Jesus and loves others. We have plenty of opportunities to love. May we all love in everything.

"More than anything else, keep watch over your heart,
since here are the wellsprings of life."

PROVERBS 4:23

A LIFE OF TRUTH AND LOVE

"In our life of truth and love, we shall have grace, mercy and peace from God the Father and from Jesus Christ, the Son of the Father."

2 JOHN 3

Because we can never be free from sin in this world, we desperately need God's grace. Because we hold on to guilt and know we fall short of God's law, we desperately need God's mercy. Because we live in a world of chaos, turmoil, and anxiousness, we desperately need the peace that can only be found in faith in God. All of the benefits of faith can find their origin in Jesus Christ alone. God is truth. God is love.

Truth. The truth is absolute and holy, constant and dependable, never-changing and eternal. The truth is we are loved by God, saved through Christ, and receive all the promises of God through faith. The truth is because we have been saved eternally, we are free to live a life abundantly confident in Him. The truth is because of Christ we are co-heirs with Him as we hold on firmly to the promise of salvation and eternal life. When we live assured of His truth, the only truth that matters, we can be confident of God's grace, mercy, and peace.

Love. Why do we love? Because He first loved us. How do we live in love? First, love God above all things, then reflect that love in every way we can. If we want God's grace, show grace to others. If we desire and long for God's mercy, be merciful and forgiving. Looking for peace? Be the source of creating peace for everyone you can. A life lived with love is a life that honors the Father and honors the Son. A life of love is an obedient life, striving to put God first and others ahead of ourselves. A real life of love has pure intentions and pure motives, always recognizing that the source of love is God Himself. Live a life of love. With all the worries and attention on the demands put on us by the world, take a deep breath and remember that grace, mercy, and peace are always close by. Feel secure in the love of the Father and find rest in the work of Christ. God is truth and God is love. Hold Him tightly and depend on Him.

"I love those who love Me;
Those who seek Me eagerly shall find Me."

PROVERBS 8:17

WHAT DO YOU WANT?

"Jesus stopped, called them over and said 'What do you want Me to do for you?'"

MATTHEW 20:32

The source of every good and perfect gift is Jesus. Jesus is the author of all that we love and cherish.

Jesus was calling over two blind men in Jericho who could not be silenced shouting out to the Lord. They knew Jesus could heal them miraculously. They were in an impossible situation, blind and shunned. But they continued their shouting, louder and louder. Lord! Lord! And He heard.

Why is it that we continue to look for worldly solutions for problems that need a Christ answer? What the world has to offer will never satisfy. Will the next set of politicians solve our problems? No. Will a pay raise or a new job give us real security? No. Will some new technology calm our souls? No. Will some new law take conflict away from our lives No. Where can we turn?

Christ tells us any problems we are experiencing are temporary and an eternity in heaven is ours for the believing. Christ tells us He has done everything necessary to save us and we can find freedom in that knowledge and hope. In Him, we are secure. Christ has fought the battle for our souls and His resurrection declares His and our victory. Christ overpowered sin, and we can find peace when we rest in that power.

Jesus healed the blind, and He can heal us as well. Their cries for the mercy of the Lord showed they believed Jesus could accomplish what the world could not. Whatever our own particular blindness is, it can be healed by our trust in Jesus. Jesus has time for each of us and even more compassion. He hears our pleas. He knows our hearts. He can heal our blindness.

So the question stands before us. What do you want Jesus to do for you? Are you willing to turn your life to Him and recognize that Jesus can do the impossible? There is no other way to salvation. His redemptive work has made us heirs with Him in eternity. He is a God that calls us to a relationship with Him in love...because He first loved us. The peace that passes all understanding can be ours when we trust our lives to Him. With the knowledge of the Good News we can live free and joyful lives, knowing our eternal futures are promised and assured.

When He asks us "what do you want me to do for you," we can reply with joy. We want what you have already done for us. We want You.

"Fear of God gives good grounds for confidence,
In Him, His children find a refuge."

PROVERBS 14:26

MORE THAN WORDS

"Why do you call me, 'Lord, Lord' and not do what I say?"

LUKE 6:46

The old saying that actions speak louder than words could not be more appropriate for this verse. Jesus is verifying that the proof in what we believe is shown by our actions and our fruits. Words come easy. A life commitment requires obedience. A life commitment continually shows growth. A life commitment tells an ongoing story about in whom and in what we truly believe.

It is easy for a Christian to let their life story end with the grace of God. Yes, our salvation is a free gift to us, bought and paid for through the blood of Jesus Christ. Yes, we are saved through faith and not by works. No, our obligations and responsibilities do not end there. The verses are numerous that remind us that our faith requires commitment and obedience on our part. We know that faith without works is dead. We know that not everyone who calls out Lord, Lord will be saved. We know in this verse that Jesus is reminding us that obedience is a requirement of our faith in no uncertain terms. We need to DO, LIVE, and SERVE because we believe that Jesus is truly Lord.

We can talk about commitment, but it is our actions that reveal our hearts. What is important, really important, to you? Is Jesus the head of your religion, or is He the king of your heart? Is God something we know about, or someone who dwells within? Do we confess Christ with our mouths, or do we witness for Christ by how we live? There is a big difference.

Obedience is essential to our relationship with Christ. It is an integral element that bears witness to placing God at the top of our priorities and the center of our hearts. Obedience is our surrender to the majesty of our Lord and Savior. Of course in this life we will never be perfect, but our willingness to DO what Christ says puts us on track to be more like Him every day, piece by piece.

All Christians have a great responsibility to honor Christ by DOING what we confess, LIVING as we believe, and WITNESSING Christ in everything that we do. The world is watching what you do much more than they are listening to what you say. The proof of our commitment is shown in every little thing we do, every day, in every circumstance. Let us all preach with our actions, doing the work that God has set before each of us. It is a life commitment to the One who gives us life. Live it.

"A man is trapped when he shouts 'Dedicated!'
And only begins to reflect after the vow."

PROVERBS 20:25

PSALM 9

Verses 1-2

Verses 9-10

"I thank You, God, with all my heart;
I recite Your marvels one by one,
I rejoice and exult in You,
I sing praise to Your name, Most high."
"May God be a stronghold for the oppressed,
A stronghold when times are hard.
Those who acknowledge Your name can rely on You,
You never desert those who seek You, God."

MY PERSPECTIVES

WHAT YOU DO

"It is not those who say to Me,
'Lord, Lord', who will enter the kingdom of heaven,
but the person who does the will of My Father in heaven."

MATTHEW 7:21

What you do speaks more clearly than your voice. How you do things reveals your motivations, priorities, and commitment. It is easy to talk, but much harder to do. So many of us are good about declaring our commitment to our Lord with our mouth, but our actions and attitudes display what is really in our hearts. God doesn't want lip service, declarations, or meaningless pageantry. He wants action, commitment, and a pure heart given to Him in service.

We are challenged every day with doing what is right in the sight of God. Every day there are opportunities to declare ourselves as children of God through the purity of our motives.

Why, then, is there a disconnect between what we know and what we do? Too often we don't see immediate consequences to our lack of godly action. Too often we put ourselves first, deciding to look the other way or ignoring our Christian responsibilities to be humble servants to Christ's commands and expectations. Too often our inaction becomes a pattern of uncaring that builds on itself until we find ourselves distanced from our relationship with God.

Our relationship with God should be the foundation for what we do. A Christian is open to the challenges of everyday life as opportunities to be servants in Christ. It is more than empathizing or identifying with those around us, it is the action and sacrifice that we make as servants in Christ that is the evidence of the will of our Father in heaven.

We should never act to get our heavenly reward, but we should act because we are already the recipients of His sacrifice and promise. Doing His will requires a life devoid of self-importance. Doing His will shapes our entire character. His will calls for pure motivation and results in a happy heart, peace, joy, and hope.

The world is full of hypocrisy. We are constantly disappointed by people who say one thing, but do something else. We continually want to show others what we want to be, but find our hearts not totally committed. Too often our actions cannot stand the test of true transparency.

Our job is to know the will of our heavenly Father, then LIVE it! A life in Jesus Christ should be described as unashamed and uncompromising. Declaring yourself a true Christian means your life shows your commitment. A Christian not only speaks the truth, they live it as well. Be firm in your convictions, declaring it daily with your actions. His promise is clear. Accept it, then LIVE IT!

"Many describe themselves as kindly men,
But who can find a man truly to be trusted?"

PROVERBS 20:6

NEVER GIVE UP

"Never give up then, my dear brothers, never admit defeat; keep on working at the Lord's work always, knowing that, in the Lord, you cannot be laboring in vain."

1 CORINTHIANS 15:58

The Lord's work always has a purpose. Sometimes the work is obvious and results are clear, and sometimes the work's purpose is hidden. This verse is one of celebration. It presents a glorious notion. In the Lord, your work cannot be in vain!

It is easy for you to become discouraged when you do not recognize the fruits of your labor. The world has its ways of diminishing your effects and ridiculing your commitment to the Lord's work. The everyday demands on your time and focus all tend to diminish the importance of your commitment to doing the Lord's work. Do not be discouraged! Never give up, never surrender! Your labors for the Lord cannot be in vain! You and your work for the Lord will reap benefits beyond your knowing.

It is impossible to work for the Lord and not have results. The power rests in Him! This verse tells us to keep on working at the Lord's work always! God has placed the opportunities and challenges before you, and it is up to us to continue His work, knowing it is all for God's purpose. Accept your daily challenges, keeping in mind that whatever you do is to the glory of God, fulfilling a need and serving a divine purpose.

Be happy in all your labors. You have a great promise that gives your work purpose. It will never be in vain. In the Lord, it cannot be in vain.

"In the day of wrath riches will be of no advantage,
but virtuous conduct delivers from death."

PROVERBS 11:4

KEEP A CALM AND SOBER MIND

"Everything will soon come to an end, so, to pray better, keep a calm and sober mind..."

1 PETER 4:7

The social physics of our society are warped. It seems the faster we try to go, the slower we get there. We desire more and more information instantaneously, only to find out that most of the information is meaningless. The demands and pace of our lives leave us searching for meaning or escape. How do we unclutter our minds and achieve a lifestyle bereft of anxiety? The answer lies in prayer. This verse doesn't say to stay calm so that you can succeed; it says to stay calm in order to pray better. We need to realize that our time here is short and there is a need in our lives to pray. We need to move the focus away from ourselves and turn to God. Everything needs perspective.

The age of modernity lacks an eternal mindset. This deficiency gets us so caught up chasing the wrong self-edifying goals and promoting our own egos that we forget that there is someone else in charge of our lives. Our minds would be so much freer if we spent as much time on our knees as we do in front of the television or computer. As much time spent in prayer as we spend in our cars would remind us of the importance of a relationship with God.

All the things that we think are so important will soon go away. Everything you think you control can disappear in the blink of an eye. Reliance on yourself leads to anxiety, turmoil, and tension. Reliance on God leads to calmness, acceptance, and peace. God doesn't want to be an afterthought or a scheduled event to check off the list. He wants a relationship and has given us the means of direct communication—prayer. He wants your mind to be focused on Him and your relationship when you are in prayer. He wants thoughtful communication. Think about what clutters your mind and what makes you anxious. Determine how important those things are. Decide what things are really important in your life. Cherish your relationship with God. Time here is short, but eternity with God can be ours.

"Simpletons have folly for their portion,
Men of discretion knowledge for their crown."

PROVERBS 14:18

THE LORD TO THE RESCUE

"The Lord will rescue me from all evil attempts on me,
and bring me safely to His heavenly kingdom.
To Him the glory for ever and ever. Amen."

2 TIMOTHY 4:18

There are many times when we can feel overwhelmed, never having enough time or patience to dwell on the right things. There are many times when it feels like we are sinking, letting the problems of the world and our circumstances pull us under. There are times when we disappoint ourselves with our lack of compassion and perspective, leaving us sorrowful and full of guilt. How can we turn away from what holds us back and flourish in a world that holds us down? In situations like this, it is Jesus to the rescue.

Need something that you can depend on that never fails? Need someone who cares for you unconditionally? Need a source of peace and rest in a troubled world? Need to find a source of power and perseverance for strength? Jesus is the answer to everything.

Jesus is our protector and guardian. He is our security and comfort. He is our strength and Savior. We are surrounded by things that can take our attention away from Him everywhere we turn. But He remains. Temptations come at us at a faster and faster pace. But He rescues us from all evil. We lose patience and let anger and anxieties have power in our lives. But He has overcome all sin and rules with love and might. Jesus to the rescue.

It is so easy to focus on the negativity around us and fail to approach life with the thankful heart that Jesus deserves. To Him be the glory. To Him be our thanks. To Him be our worship. As we stay in Him, He provides the security, peace, and contentment that we so desperately need in this world. Lift your head above the waters that surround you, and grab on to the hand of Jesus. He will save you now and for eternity. Jesus to the rescue.

"To be afraid of men is a snare,
He who puts his trust in God is secure."

PROVERBS 29:25

HOLY HANDS

"I want men everywhere to lift up holy hands in prayer, without anger or disputing."

1 TIMOTHY 2:8

God wants all of us to set aside our temporal differences and unite in prayer. How often are our hands holy? Is your conscience clear when you pray? Anger distorts our thoughts and our selfishness changes our perspectives. God's message is pure and holy. All of our earthly cares can be brought before Him without the need for anger.

God unites. We divide. Our lack of tolerance can be so divisive. There is only one God, and He knows our heart. He can see our anger and the ungodliness of our hands. We need to be cleansed through the sacrifice of Christ to have our hands made Holy. This means Christ must be at our center and the power of His grace must be accepted for us to pray with Holy hands. What a blessing this is!

Let God take the anger from your soul today. Let God reveal a pathway toward the resolution of your disputes. When you pray today, do so with Holy hands, washed clean by the grace of God. Be united in faith with all believers, having the peace of mind that only God gives. Focus on the unity that God brings and do not give priority to the differences we have among us here on earth. Let God make your hands Holy, then honor Him with your prayers.

"Hatred provokes disputes,
love covers over all offenses."

PROVERBS 10:12

THE PROPER TIME

"We must never get tired of doing good because if we don't give up the struggle we shall get our harvest at the proper time."

GALATIANS 6:9

Timing is everything. How often do we get frustrated when life doesn't happen on our timetable? How powerless do we feel when we don't get the results we want when we want them? We are very good at scheduling, expectations, and goals but oftentimes very weak on patience. It is so difficult to look at what lays before us every day as part of the larger picture of completeness in Christ. While we continually check our watches and calendars, God's timing is eternal. We often cannot see how events and decisions we make today will affect our futures. But God's timing is perfect.

We have a very important directive from Paul in this verse...never tire of doing good. Goodness and love should be part of our nature in the present, in every circumstance that is in front of us. It is a directive that doesn't depend on circumstances or convenience. The struggle to always do good is worth the price, because the reward is so great. Purposeful acts of goodness demonstrate that we trust a God who first loved us and promises an eternity with Him. It demonstrates that we are not slaves to circumstance, but instead free in Christ to be a witness of God's grace. God's timing is perfect.

In Paul's letter to the Galatians, he speaks to the freedom and liberty that we as believers have in Christ. We are free to do good. We are free to love. We are free to show charity. We are free to let God be God. God does not promise that life will be easy or that we will not have to struggle. But we are to never give up! We are to never compromise our faith and trust in Him! Never tire of doing good! God's timing is perfect.

What we can trust unreservedly in is God's timing. God is in charge and His promises are true. His plan for each of us is to do good at every opportunity and in every circumstance that He has right in front of us every day, letting us rely on both our harvest and His timing. He develops character and patience as we trust God in every situation. God has a plan and time for each of us. Be sure you are ready to do good...always.

"A man's heart plans out his way
But it is God who makes his steps secure."

PROVERBS 16:9

PSALM 145

Verses 10-13

"God, all Your creatures thank You,
And Your faithful bless You.
Kingly and glorious they proclaim You,
They affirm Your might.
Let mankind learn Your acts of power,
And the majestic glory of Your sovereignty!
Your sovereignty is an eternal sovereignty,
Your empire lasts from age to age."

MY PERSPECTIVES

CHRIST IN ME

"And I live now not with my own life but with the life of Christ who lives in me. The life I now live in this body I live in faith: faith in the Son of God who loved me and who sacrificed Himself for my sake."

GALATIANS 2:20

The life of a Christian is, in many ways, a life of inversion, a life lived from the inside out. It is the person of Christ that dwells in the heart that dictates the actions, attitudes, and faith of the believer. It is our testimony to the heart of Christ when we live in His grace and freedom to let ourselves be used for His purposes. When we let Christ be our guide we can live without fear, reservation, or doubt. When Christ lives inside, we can live with an abundance of joy, peace, and trust. The suffering and death of Christ was for each of us. The resurrection of Christ is our assurance of His promises. His death led to our life. Let Him live in you as you live in Him.

Each of us should ask ourselves how connected we are to Christ. Are we ruled by sin and subject to molding our attitudes to appease the world? Or did we participate in the victory over sin with Christ in His resurrection? Are we on a constant search to find happiness in a world full of hardship? Or does our source of joy come from faith in a conquering Christ? Do we judge our success on a bank account, stature in the community, or the things that we have? Or is our worth based on the love shown through Christ as He suffered for us, shares His grace with us, and desires a relationship with us. With Christ inside, there is always abundance. With Christ inside, there is always love. With Christ inside, there is always compassion. Let Him fill you up.

Our worth and value is made plain because Christ sacrificed for us. He gave Himself up for something important...you. He suffered to provide an eternity of peace...for you. He claims victory over sin...for you. His amazing grace is His gift...for you. Live life from the inside out, acknowledging and celebrating that Christ is at your core. He is alive! He is alive in you! Live like it!

"More than all else, keep watch over your heart,
Since here are the wellsprings of life."

PROVERBS 4:23

THE VALUE OF SOLITUDE

"...but He would always go off to some place where he could be alone and pray."

LUKE 5:16

Do you feel overwhelmed by the time constraints and demands in your life? Are you attached to your cell phone to the point where you can't stand the thought of being disconnected? Is your mind so engaged with the day-to-day that there is no room for silence? Jesus knew the value of full focus on the Father. Do you?

The pace of life is growing exponentially. As a result, the demands grow at the same rate. The more we use technology to simplify our lives, the more we become slaves to its presence. In a world of constant connection, we are the losers. We thrive on instant information and instant gratification instead of deep relationships. We were promised a simpler life, yet our calendars get fuller and fuller. We have let a fast-paced world invade our intimacy with God.

No one who has ever lived had the demands on their life like Jesus. Throngs came to Him to be healed. Multitudes yearned for His presence. The nation of Israel longed for a conquering king. He carried daily the weight of a sinful world. Yet He found value and necessity in finding a time to be alone. Even Jesus needed to be in a condition that would allow intimacy with the Father. Even Jesus knew that His relationship with the Father was greater than what the world around Him was demanding. Even Jesus needed time to focus and be in communion. Even Jesus.

When do you find time for the Father? Not a few seconds squeezed in between appointments, but a time for real conversation. When we lay out our day, does God come first, or only if there is time left over? Do you squeeze God into your life, or let life revolve around Him? Jesus knew His strength and view of His calling was directly tied to the Father. He gave Him time. He gave Him focused time. He gave Him priority. He gave Himself. And He prayed.

Today's advances and tomorrow's fascinations may be newsworthy and the talk of the day, but they do not replace prayer. The newest "must have" cannot replace the real "must have," God. We must have God. It must be important. It is commonly said a Christian is in this world but not of this world. Can you separate the two? Can you set all the world has to offer aside and lean on what God has to offer? Can you be alone with God? Only in that space can you gauge your relationship and dependence on Him. Step back, be silent, be alone, and pray with Him.

"Listen, my son, and learn to be wise,
And guide your heart in the way."

PROVERBS 23:22

BE A TEMPLE FOR GOD

"The temple of God has no common ground with idols, and that is what we are–the temple of the living God."

2 CORINTHIANS 6:16

There is no debate, no compromise, no tolerance, no rationalization. God does not share space, allegiance, or identity with idols. Can you call yourself a temple of God? What dwells inside you: God or idols? There is no place for both at the same time! We are called to be the dwelling of His Holy Spirit and that does not leave any space for idols.

What is important to you? Are you aware of the "idols" that influence your behavior? Idols cry out to us for attention and a home every day. Our lack of contentment and pride pushes us to covet more and more material things, filling our days with a pursuit of our own accomplishments. We spend our waking hours wanting and working for more and more, not realizing that God has done everything for us that is truly important.

Are you a temple for the living God? Is God filling you so completely that there is room for nothing else? Examine yourself to see what gets in the way of the humbleness needed to be a temple for God. Determine what your motives are and see if you value relationships over material goods, others over yourself, and God's plan for your life over plans of your own.

Idols take every shape and form imaginable. Our priorities and motives reveal so much about our faith and the amount of space in us that belongs to God. We worship something all the time throughout the day. Our actions show who or what it is that we worship and what we feel is important. Does your life exhibit the peace and assurance that only God can give? Is your temple one that shows the world that God is dwelling there? God is not just another god to be brought out at our convenience and to be called upon to meet our own agenda. God is God. There is no other! Anything else is an idol, a fraudulent evil not worthy to be in the same place as God.

Think of the power that resides within you when God is inside you! The highest honor and responsibility is ours to be a worthy dwelling place for the Almighty God. What a privilege and honor we have! Realize what the world makes important and push these "idols" away from yourself. Realize the importance and power of God and open yourself to Him. God will fill you beyond your hopes and understanding. Be His temple!

"I love those who love Me;
Those who seek Me eagerly shall find Me."

PROVERBS 8:17

TO SAVE SINNERS

"Here is a saying that you can rely on and nobody should doubt; that Christ Jesus came into the world to save sinners. I myself am the greatest of them..."

1 TIMOTHY 1:15

The salvation that Christ brought to this world is not a theory or story. It is a fact. This salvation is not a wish or hope. It is real. This salvation is not a piece of folklore. It is the truth. Jesus did not just show up on earth, there was an eternal purpose. This verse helps put into focus the entire Gospel. If we use this verse as a foundational lens, everything comes into focus. He came with a heavenly purpose, sacrificed to cover the entirety of sin, and accomplished that for the benefit of each of us personally. It reminds us that it is Christ's work, despite our sinful nature and sinful actions, which comes from the fullness of God's love. We did not earn this gift, but on the contrary, He gives the gift of salvation from grace. He loved us first.

Who is the sinner? Me. You. All of mankind has sinned and fallen short of the glory of God. No one can claim Christ only to themselves, as He came so that no one would be left out from His gracious gift. There is no classification of a better sinner as superior to a worse sinner. We all have sinned and fall short, needing the redeeming blood of Christ to cleanse us. When we are inclined to look at the sin of others and compare our relative "goodness," it is helpful to look at how Paul viewed himself. Let us never lose sight of the fact that we each need the grace that Christ has provided just as much as everyone else. Our boasting should be in the Lord.

What is the cost of this? To Christ, the cost is His blood and sacrifice on the cross. To me and you, it is at no cost, merely the acceptance of the gift of His grace. Christ's blood covers all sin equally and eternally. That covering is ours for the believing. That covering helps us recognize ourselves as sinners, gives us the awareness of our need to repent, and helps us follow Christ faithfully. With our faithful acceptance comes the freedom to live as a saved soul, living with confidence in the power of God. Christ came to this world to save me, to save you, to save all those who believe. Praise God.

"What man can say, 'I have cleansed my heart,
I am purified of my sin'?"

PROVERBS 20:9

KEEP GROWING

"Instead, go on growing in the grace and in the knowledge
of our Lord and Savior Jesus Christ.
To Him be glory, in time and in eternity.
Amen."

2 PETER 3:18

Faith is a journey. Faith increases the more we use it. Through that faith we can grow closer and closer to our Savior Jesus Christ. Our faith life is a road that has many turns, challenging us to stay on course. It has its ups and downs, requiring us to stay focused on Him to stay grounded and faithful in Him. As we mature in our understanding, reliance, and faith in God, we will face obstacles. But He is true. Jesus is dependable. He is worthy. Never stop growing.

There are many things that happen in our lives that don't make sense until much later. The twists and turns of life sometimes seem pointless and meaningless until everything fits together. It is all part of growth. The more we depend on God and the longer view that we take, the more that His love and presence are visible in our lives. To grow we need to feed ourselves with His Word. To grow we need to communicate with Him in prayer. To grow we need to see His hand more and more active in our lives and follow wherever He leads. To grow we need to focus more and more on Him. It is a process.

God is a God of abundance. He always has more for us in mind as we strive to follow Him in our daily lives. He has another piece of understanding, another glimpse of His majesty, and another stirring of our heart ahead. He has a path we may not see or understand, a blessing around the next corner, and an opportunity for us to love just ahead. He expects us to grow. His grace will lead the way.

God is always present in the moment, but is also God of eternity. The constancy of God is something we can hold on to with trust and assurance. If we have a mind to constantly move toward God, then difficulties become opportunities, setbacks become times for reflection, and disappointments can humble us to set ourselves aside and wait for His grace. We grow in Him when we accept His grace through faith and strive to know Him more and more. The glory is His, now and forever. Grow and let yourself thrive in His grace.

"The path of the virtuous is like the light of dawn,
Its brightness growing to the fullness of day."

PROVERBS 4:18

WHOM DO YOU PLEASE?

"So now whom am I trying to please—man, or God? Would you say it is men's approval I am looking for? If I still wanted that, I should not be what I am—a servant of Christ."

GALATIANS 1:10

Who do you try to please: man or God? Paul makes his position clear! As a servant of Christ, he will please God. Are you a servant of Christ? I am sure that we want to answer a resounding "yes," but do our actions back up our servanthood? A true servant of Christ should demonstrate the qualities that Christ displayed. Does your life show humbleness, faithfulness, and integrity? Would you be described as gracious, caring, and courageous? Are you truly willing to put Christ ahead of your ambitions and become His servant?

The world often has different values. From a secular standpoint, success requires pride and ostentatious wealth. We want power and try to obtain it by putting others down. Status, position, and possessions take up so much of our time and effort. Ambition is applauded.

Where is your ambition directed? Do your efforts and your use of your time reveal what is important in your life? Let us take up a new goal, to be a servant of Christ. Let us stop the chase for worldly goods and the slavery that it demands. Break out of the trappings of this world and find true freedom. Christ came full of power, but chose to live as a sacrifice in humility. He had everything at His hands, but chose to bear the costs of your sins to give us the gift of eternal life. We turned our back on Him, yet He chose to forgive us.

Our declaration should be the same as Paul's to the Galatians. "What I am—a servant of Christ" changes everything. As servants, we are free to receive all that Christ has done for us. As servants, we are free to do God's work here on earth, trusting a living God. We no longer need to measure ourselves by the world's standards, but instead by the closeness of our relationship with God. In all areas of our lives, we must recognize whom we are trying to please. Do you want true peace and freedom? Become a servant of Christ.

"He who listens closely to the Word shall find happiness;
He who puts his trust in God is blessed."

PROVERBS 16:20

PSALM 91

Verses 14-16

"I rescue all who cling to Me,
I protect whoever knows My name,
I answer everyone who invokes Me,
I am with them when they are in trouble;
I bring them safety and honor.
I give them life, long and full,
And show them how I can save."

MY PERSPECTIVES

ALL THAT WE NEED

"By His divine power, He has given us all the things that we need for life and for true devotion, bringing us to know God Himself, who has called us by His own glory and goodness."

2 PETER 1:3

All that you need is yours! All that you need to know God Himself is before you. Why do we spend so much of our time searching when the true gift is before us? You cannot think your way to devotion. It is by His divine power that you have received the gifts of life and devotion. His power grants you relationship with God. God Himself has called you!

The questions for us regarding how we obtain these gifts are found in the verses following 2 Peter 1:3, and we are challenged to mature our faith by depending on God. Will you add your goodness to the faith that you have? Will you add understanding to your goodness? Will you add self-control to your understanding, patience to your self-control, true devotion to your patience, and kindness to your devotion?

If you are willing to say yes to these questions, your life will change. Your attitude and perceptions will change. You will find peace. His divine power has made it all possible. To answer yes and follow through on a commitment to God requires His power for true devotion. Accept the gifts of life and devotion that God has put before you. The gifts are right in front of you. Stop searching. Accept, believe, and live the promises of God. Only then can you truly know God Himself.

"When a man has a ready answer he has joy too,
how satisfying is the apt reply."

PROVERBS 15:23

THE PROMISE

"...Scripture makes no exceptions when it says that sin is master everywhere. In this way the promise can only be given through faith in Jesus Christ and can only be given to those who have this faith."

GALATIANS 3:22

Do you think you can conquer sin by yourself? Do you think you can stop sinning? Do you think there are multiple ways to receive the promise of salvation? Think again.

This verse makes it very clear that there is no way that we can master sin. Left on our own, we will sin over and over again, despite our best efforts. We cannot be good enough, generous enough, or well-intentioned enough. None of us are special enough to not have sin be part of our experience. We should never be surprised by sin...it is everywhere. But the good news, The Promise, is that Jesus Christ brings life. He has done what we cannot do, conquer sin. He has made possible an eternal answer to our temporary predicaments. This answer is ours if we only believe in Christ. Only Christ brings freedom from the perils and mastery of sin in this world. Only Christ justifies us so that we can be full recipients of the grace of God.

There is also only one way to receive this marvelous freedom, and that is through faith in Christ. Too often we put faith in ourselves thinking we can control our sinful natures. Even though sin is around every corner, it can serve a godly purpose. It forces us to realize that we need to depend on the saving grace of Christ and not ourselves. The mastery of Christ overcomes the mastery of sin always, and we can receive that victory through faith in Him. Even in a broken world, we can know that God's plan and promise for our salvation is true through faith in Christ. It is His plan for us.

Hope, joy, and assuredness await those with faith in Christ, no matter what the circumstance. Eternal salvation is promised through faith in Christ and no other way. His way is perfect. His way is available. His way is for everyone through faith. Let loose of yourself and grab firmly onto the faith in Christ that conquers sin. The Promise is ours through faith.

"What man can say, 'I have cleansed my heart,
I am purified of my sin'?"

PROVERBS 20:9

LIFE MEANS MORE

"That is why I am telling you not to worry about your life and what you are to eat, nor about your body and how you are to clothe it. Surely life means more than food, and the body more than clothing."

MATTHEW 6:25

Our own meaning of life and the constantly escaping feeling of self-satisfaction that goes along with it leads to worry. God's meaning of life and the joy that goes with it leads to peace. We are about things; He is about relationships. We strive to store things up, depending on ourselves. He wants us to use His gifts for the benefit of others, depending on Him to meet our needs. We worry. He rejoices.

This verse puts life into perspective. It emphasizes that life is so much more when we stop worrying and turn our eyes to Him. Everyday challenges are changed to possibilities. Exasperations are turned into patience. Disappointments are transformed into hope.

So much of our time is spent trying to fulfill our narrow idea of what is important. We want more and more, thinking that happiness is something measured by quantity. Life is so much more! Here God is telling us that He has our necessities covered. He is telling us that the life He has intended for us is full and rich. Our focus should be on relationships rather than material goods.

The spirit of worry can be so divisive. Worrying changes outlooks and reasoning, attitudes and priorities, reactions and motivations. Worrying steals a relationship with God. This verse is about trust, trusting God to take care of you. It is about relying on Him rather than ourselves. It is about putting God first. It is about finding peace.

Don't let worrying drive a wedge between you and the Lord. Be aware of the differences between needs and wants. God will take care of your needs. Your life is precious to Him. Rely on Him.

"Better a dry crust and with it peace,
Than a house where feast and dispute go together."

PROVERBS 17:1

UNLOAD YOUR WORRIES

"...Unload all our worries onto Him, since He is looking after you."

1 PETER 5:7

How do you handle your worries? Today's society would teach you coping mechanisms for them, or prescribe a bottle of pills, or it might outright tell you to ignore them. The world tells you that surely there is something you can do to relieve your stress and depression. Perhaps practicing positive thinking will overpower your worries. If all else fails, find someone to blame for your problems. These are worldly practices and not what the Bible teaches!

The world's answers do not acknowledge that God is looking after you. He is watching out for you! We are not the answer, God is. Trusting only yourself leads to more anxiety and more disappointment. Trusting God brings peace and fulfillment. This verse does not tell us to deal with our worries, it tells us to unload them. Our worries are no longer ours when we give them to God. We must give our worries away, casting them away from us, and trust God to deal with them. God can handle our worries, without Him we cannot. It all comes down to how much you trust God to take care of you. We so desperately want to be in control of our own circumstances and future that we forget how little power we really have.

If God is looking after you, why do you worry? Someone who trusts God without reservation gives no power to worry. Your eternity is secure and the inconveniences and worries you have now pale in comparison to the promises of God. Whatever we deal with, God will take care of us. What great freedom this gives! How differently would you live your life if worry was not part of it? How much energy and time do you spend worrying? How directly influenced is the way you live your life by worry? Give your worries to God. Do not hold on to any of them. Live with confidence, knowing that God is looking out for you. He knows you and will provide for you in His divine wisdom. We have no idea what tomorrow might bring, but we do know that God will be by our side, watching out for us. God does not want us to spend our time here on earth worrying. He wants us to live as His children, full of trust and faith. Unload your worries and live!

"Worry makes a man's heart heavy,
a kindly word makes it glad."

PROVERBS 12:25

HE IS WITH ME

"He who sent Me is with Me, and has not left Me to Myself, for I always do what pleases Him."

JOHN 8:29

Who is God to you? Is He with you? Do you feel His presence with you now? Sometimes? Never? It is so easy to know about God, yet not realize He is always with you. Too often God becomes more of a concept and something "out there" to many of us, and we lose touch with the personal presence of God. When things get hard, remember…He is with you. When you feel lonely, remember…He has not left you to yourself. What a great comfort it is to have a loving God with us, no matter what.

There are times when we think of God as a resident of a church or someone far away who might listen to a prayer if we send one. We live our own lives, calling on God only when things get out of control. We let sin creep in and push God away. We put ourselves ahead of faith. But despite what we do, we are still loved and never alone. God is there.

An important transformation for the believer is when we stop living for God and start living with God. He is here. He is real. He is with us every step of the way. He is consistent, even when we are not. He loves even when we fail. His arm is around us in our doubts and in our despair. He sits with us in times of sorrow and fear. He is merciful even when we are selfish. He is always there, even in our loneliness.

Who is God? My life. Is He with me? Always. When we look deeply into ourselves, we know that God is the source of trust, comfort, faith, and grace. He is with us. He is on our side. His power will save us.

I do not have the power to save myself. But God does have the power. He is with me, His strength is greater than anything, and His motives are pure. He loves me. And that love is with me wherever I go and always present. He is with me.

"In every course you take, have Him in mind:
He will see that your paths are smooth."

PROVERBS 3:6

GO NEAR TO GOD

"The nearer you go to God, the nearer He will come to you."

JAMES 4:8

Have you ever wondered why you didn't feel close to God, or why He maybe doesn't seem real? Have you been striving to get nearer to Him? So many things seem so important to us, and we want to identify ourselves with the "importance" of the world. God wants a relationship and is always available to us if we seek a relationship with Him.

God is not just a tool to be used by us when we find ourselves in trouble. God is not to be kept on a shelf to be pulled down by us when we need divine intervention in our lives. God wants to be your God every day of the week, not just Sundays and religious holidays. He wants to be included in every part of our lives, not just during a quick prayer before we indulge in a meal. God wants a relationship.

This verse tells us that there is action and commitment required by us. The key word in the first part of the verse is "go." It doesn't say the more you think about God, or the more you behave, or the more you need God. It says the nearer you GO. Are you actively seeking God, wanting more than anything else to go where He is to be in close relationship with Him?

The second part of the verse fills us with promise. He will come near to you! It bears repeating, God wants a relationship! So often we ask why we feel that God has deserted us or why God seems to disappear from our lives. Perhaps He is waiting for you to appear to Him. He is waiting, ready to fulfill His promise of relationship with you. Are you ready to go?

We expect so much from God, but find it hard to commit to the journey to Him. I will ask again, are you ready to go? What level of commitment are you ready to make to go nearer to God? How far will you go? Think about committing all aspects of your life to your journey to Him. Be ready to find that close relationship with Him. He promises He will come.

"The name of God is a strong tower,
The virtuous man runs to it and is secure."

PROVERBS 18:10

PSALM 33

Verses 17-22

"But see how the eye of God is on those who fear Him,
On those who rely on His love,
To rescue their souls from death
and keep them alive in famine.
Our soul awaits God,
He is our help and shield;
Our hearts rejoice in Him,
We trust in His holy name.
God, let Your love rest on us
As our hope has rested in You."

MY PERSPECTIVES

WISDOM FROM ABOVE

"Whereas the wisdom that comes down from above is essentially something pure; it also makes for peace, and is kindly and considerate; it is full of compassion and shows itself by doing good; nor is there any trace of partiality or hypocrisy in it."

JAMES 3:17

Information in more volume and in more depth than ever before is flooding us. We do not have the lack of information; we have the lack of knowledge and understanding of how to use that information. We make snap decisions, base our decisions on analytics, and put our faith in data. Too often we miss the real goal...to act with the wisdom given us through faith. It is the wisdom that comes from above that gives value to what we know and pure purpose to what we do. We need to spend less time looking at data and more time experiencing the wisdom that God provides.

God's wisdom does not have a worldly motive, but instead has a motive to actively put love into action. His wisdom is pure, always meant for encouragement and to uplift the spirit. His wisdom finds a way toward peace, pushing aside differences and focusing on what brings us all as His created creatures together. His love for us is the most compelling unifying force the world has ever seen. I love the word 'compassion' because it speaks perfectly to the essence of God.

In His compassion for us He reveals Himself as the source of mercy and understanding. Through His grace and forgiveness He shows how concerned and loving He is for each of us. His compassion is for everyone, giving all His creation a pathway to salvation. He lets us not just know about Him, but to know Him and experience His pure, compassionate wisdom.

So how do we respond to this heavenly wisdom? How can we find peace in the midst of conflict? How can we find a way to ease the suffering of others? How can we back away from a world that competes for our attention and glorifies wealth and self? How do we accept the wisdom from above and commit to putting God first? Do good. In every situation and at every opportunity put the wisdom from above into personal action. No judgments and no partiality. We are called to simply do good, be pure in our motivation, and be considerate and kind to every single person we meet. We are an agent of His wisdom when we are obedient to His will and listen to Him before we act. We reflect His wisdom when we act with compassion. We let our lives testify to His wisdom when we are kind and considerate.

This world needs to listen and put into action the wisdom of God more than ever. We can play our part, actively seeking His wisdom and acting to promote His love. When the world tries to separate us, we can bind together in His love. When we see anger and anxiousness, we can seek peace and harmony. The wisdom from above can guide us as we use what we know to trust in the God of purity, peace, equality, and compassion.

"Tuning your ear to wisdom, and applying your heart to truth."

PROVERBS 2:2

"You will then understand what the fear of God is,
and discover the knowledge of God."

PROVERBS 2:5

THE TRUTH WILL MAKE YOU FREE

"If you make my word your home you will indeed be my disciples, you will learn the truth and the truth will make you free."

JOHN 8:31-32

Where do you live? What do you call home? Is it just a place, or does it represent your authentic self? Your home is where your heart is. Is your heart committed completely to the Word? Does your heart find its rest and purpose in the Word? Do you do everything you can to make your heart a place for the Word to reside and prosper? Apart from God, have you ever felt really free? These are hard questions, but they reveal much about where we truly put our trust.

The basic concept of the character of Christ is found in this verse. His Word is truth. His Word is not part of a larger picture or simply a suggestion. It is truth. We live in a world that doesn't tolerate the truth of the Bible. It is scorned as theology that hinders ambitions and motives. We look everywhere to find something to depend on, when Jesus is there all the time, waiting and ready to provide a life of freedom. We trust in ourselves, willing to bend the rules or rationalize our behavior, instead of accepting the pure truth that Jesus provides. We focus on the pursuit of material things which only enslaves us, instead of looking to Jesus and the freedom that comes from relying on His grace and love. We look in all the wrong places when we already have Jesus, the ultimate source of truth and freedom.

It is ironic how hard we make life. We make it all about ourselves, yet we are never at peace and always in search of more. But Jesus makes it easy. He has done the work for you. It is in Him and His truth that we can live without fear, without anxiety, and without regret. He and He alone set us free to love completely, trust completely, and find real peace. These are benefits for the heart, where your home is, depending on the truth of His Word. While turmoil surrounds us, our heart and home can be at peace. With the clamor going on around us, yelling for our allegiance, we can rest in the knowledge that our leader, Jesus, is the only one with all the answers. While more and more rules and regulations pile up against us, our hearts and homes remain free to love tirelessly and patiently when Jesus is our real authority.

Images and ideas come at us fast in this world and they show no sign of slowing. Rhetoric and conflict continue to escalate when the world pushes God away. There is no freedom apart from God. We can have a different path. We can keep our eyes focused on Jesus and be His disciple, pulling God closer instead of pushing Him away. We can look to the Word instead of man to mold our lives. We can live without fear when we trust God to be our provider, authority, and salvation. We have the Truth. We have the Word. We have Jesus. Live in the freedom that comes from a heart and home full of God.

"Like the bird that strays from its nest,
So is the man who strays from where he belongs."

PROVERBS 27:8

HUNGER AND THIRST

"I am the bread of life, He who comes to me will never be hungry; he who believes in me will never thirst."

JOHN 6:35

There is a lot of effort and conversation about what we should put into our bodies. The right amount of carbs, fats, and protein seem to be very important. We want to be as healthy as possible, trying desperately to defeat aging and mortality. While this is important, it pales in comparison to what spiritual food we need. We need a new focus on eternal food. We need Christ.

We hunger for so many things in this world. We hunger for comfort, prestige, position, and money. We hunger for relationships and self-worth. We hunger for peace and joy. The problem is we too often look to the wrong source to satisfy us. The world cannot provide the bread that we need. We need Christ.

We thirst for knowledge. We thirst for reason. We thirst for justice. We thirst for importance. We continually seek out ways for our basic needs to be met. The world cannot quench our thirst. We are parched, yet we too seldom look for the true source that will refresh us. We need Christ.

The good news is that the food for our souls that Jesus promises never runs out. You will NEVER be hungry. You will NEVER thirst. The spiritual food that we need is ours in abundance and is available to us whenever we need it. It is the source of our strength and endurance. It builds us up and sustains us. It is eternal.

Christ is the foundation for our existence. He provides the right amount of everything for our bodies and our souls. He gives us life and lets us live it to its fullest. He is the provider of our strength and fortitude, our energy and joy. Busy counting calories? Count your blessings instead. Busy reading food package labels? Read the Word instead. Trying to schedule another exercise class? Exercise your love for God first. Devoting yourself to a new daily schedule? Be sure to schedule in God for the first fruits of your attention.

We can only be a shell of what we were created to be without realizing that Christ is the source of our existence. He is the ultimate provider, knowing what our true needs are and then meeting our needs. He loves, provides, and sustains us. Instead of a healthy dose of vitamins, get a healthy dose of Christ. Your cupboard will never be bare and you will never be out of water when Christ provides.

"The fear of God leads to life,
A man has food and shelter, and no evil to fear."

PROVERBS 19:23

CONSEQUENCES

"In other words, since they refused to see it was rational to acknowledge God, God left them to their own irrational idea and to their monstrous behavior."

ROMANS 1:28

Man always thinks he has a better idea. Man wants everything on his terms and cannot come to grips with the truth that God is sovereign over everything. The further we get from the acknowledgment of God, the further we slip into monstrous behavior.

Society condones ungodly behavior rather than confronting it. Absolute truth is becoming a foreign concept. We rationalize our ungodly behavior to the point where we have convinced ourselves that there are degrees of truth that are adaptable to different situations. Every day our society takes another step away from acknowledging God as it strives to become completely secular.

A life in Jesus is not a part-time commitment. We cannot insert God into a situation only when we see fit or it meets our needs.

Mankind has been on a steady course away from God and toward itself, thinking our body is our own and we will judge for ourselves what is right and wrong. What fools we are! God is God! The simple act of acknowledging

His existence should change the way we act and think. Without God, man's ideas are self-serving. Without God, our goals consist of material wealth, self-importance, self-protection, and advancement. Where do these ideals take us? They take us directly to the monstrous behavior of our own making.

We have every opportunity to acknowledge God. His miracles and creations are around us every day, yet we look for other explanations. His Word reveals how we should live, yet we depend on secular, situational truth to define and justify our actions. We are surrounded by monstrous behavior which surely saddens God.

So what do we do? Is there hope? Absolutely, and it begins with acknowledging God's existence, power, compassion, and promises. We need to acknowledge that God is real and active in our lives. We need to commit to living for Him. It is time to stand up for God and acknowledge Him as our redeemer and the only hope for the world. Once we put our faith in Him, we can leave our monstrous behavior behind. Acknowledge Him and let Him fill you, change you, and save you.

"The godless is forever coveting,
The virtuous man gives without ever refusing."

PROVERBS 21:26

THINK

"Think before you do anything–hold on to what is good and avoid every form of evil."

1 THESSALONIANS 5:21-22

Hindsight is a fickle thing. How many mistakes could have been avoided? How many situations could we have made better? How many chances to witness for Christ have been missed needlessly if only we would have been intentional in our approach before acting? Every day we are faced with choices that require an evaluation, choice, and action. Too often we make those decisions more difficult than they need to be. It really is very basic. This verse breaks it down to three directives that will make our lives so much simpler, content, and a reflection of the character of Christ.

First, we must think. God has blessed each of us with the ability to discern right from wrong, good from evil. He did not create us to be purely reactive, but instead to act responsibly with empathy and understanding. Our actions should be thoughtful and purposeful, reasonable and faithful. Do not let impulses dictate your actions, but instead be guided by the wisdom that God provides you.

Second, we must hold fast to what is good. Goodness is precious and pure. Goodness is well-intended and sacrificial. Goodness is humble and kind. Goodness embodies the character of God and displays a relationship with Him. Look for goodness in all situations, ensuring that your motivations are pure. Goodness can sustain you and can be a source of true peace and contentment. Claim the goodness that surrounds you, and take nothing for granted.

Last, we must avoid evil at every cost. This verse does not say tolerate or excuse evil, but instead avoid it! Actively distance yourself from evil and have nothing to do with it. Place yourself and your behavior clearly and completely on the side of goodness. So many times we rationalize and explain our behavior based on circumstances rather than what we know to be right. Take yourself away from situations or circumstances that have the potential for evil, and instead find a home with God.

The decisions and actions we take require sound thinking, trust in God, discipline, and commitment. Continually pray for God's wisdom and the strength to do what is pleasing to Him.

"For God Himself is giver of wisdom,
From His mouth issues knowledge and discernment."

PROVERBS 2:6

THE FACT IS

"The fact is, brothers, and I want you to realize this, the Good News preached is not a human message that I was given by men, it is something I learnt only through a revelation of Jesus Christ."

GALATIANS 1:11-12

Fact: Something that actually exists; truth; known to be true

The Good News preached is not a man-made solution, a wish list, or a mystical interpretation. It is fact! In this verse to the Galatians, Paul declares that the salvation message he was preaching is the result of direct communication with Christ and was not dependent upon human input or ideas. The truth of the Good News is the absolute truth! Nothing man can add and no human stipulation can interfere with the saving grace of God. No requirement beyond the suffering, death, and resurrection of Christ was necessary or valid. Paul gives the unadulterated facts of salvation to a community who were starting to add their own stipulations to be saved and questioning Paul's authority. Paul's authority comes directly from Christ. Paul reminds them that Christ is the final authority.

It is unfortunate that man seems to want to find a way to interject himself into the plan of salvation from God. We want to put on restrictions and contingencies, value practices over faith, and make God fit into our idea of how we should be saved. But fact is fact. Truth is truth. The Good News is God's alone.

God's plan is real. It is not as complicated as we want to make it. It is the truth. It is a fact. Faith in something larger than ourselves is sometimes a difficult task. We want to control every aspect of our lives and forget that God has planned for our lives all along. He knows you, He knows where you are physically and spiritually, and He knows your heart. God has already given you everything you need through the Good News of Jesus Christ. That truth is a fact. God exists. He is real. Experience it.

"For God Himself is giver of wisdom,
From His mouth issue knowledge and discernment."

PROVERBS 2:6

PSALM 31

Verses 1-3

“In You, God, I take shelter;
Never let me be disgraced.
In Your righteousness deliver me, rescue me,
Turn Your ear to me, make haste!
Be a sheltering rock for me,
A walled fortress to save me!t
For You are my rock, my fortress;
For the sake of Your name, guide me, lead me!”

MY PERSPECTIVES

THROUGH GRACE

"When we were dead through our sins, He brought us to life with Christ—it is through grace that you have been saved."

EPHESIANS 2:5

Grace is a hard concept for us to comprehend. We prefer outcomes that are both expected and practical as a result of our decisions. It is comfortable to us when our actions deliver a consequential result. We are told hard work will be rewarded and pride in our work will make us successful. When it comes to our salvation, we too often miss what is important. Jesus.

God has chosen to love us, despite our sin. God has chosen to save us because our salvation is what He desires. God has chosen to forgive us, even though we do not deserve His mercy. While all these options do not come easy to us, they are the absolute essence of God. He is grace. He is mercy. He is forgiveness. He is love. All of Him is ours through faith.

A salvation based on works would be a salvation never obtained. We cannot be good enough to earn salvation. We cannot try harder, put in more hours, or try to out-give God. When we fall short, He overcomes. When we fail, He is victorious. When we are at our weakest, He is strong and able. When we feel alone, He is present and compassionate. How blessed we are to have a God who has chosen to show His majesty by choosing to give us a path to salvation and a way to eternal life with Him. His work, His way, because He is God. Accept His grace with faith and be alive, be saved, and be thankful. He never fails.

"He who listens closely to the word shall find happiness;
He who puts his trust in God is blessed."

PROVERBS 16:20

BE A HOME FOR CHRIST

"Let the message of Christ, in all its richness, find a home with you."

COLOSSIANS 3:16

There is a difference between being a house for Christ and being a home for Christ. A house is a structure. A home is an experience. Is your relationship with Christ a structure that allows yourself to identify with Christ? Or is it an experience with Christ that allows the full richness of His blessing to be enjoyed?

The message of Christ reveals itself in every phase of your life when you are His home. The world demands that we separate our politics, tolerance, and decisions from our faith. We are told that religion has no place when it comes to making decisions. How false it is! There is no way to separate ourselves from Christ when He finds His home within us. Every decision, every action, every motivation comes from a mindset of service, sacrifice, and obedience when we let the richness of Christ inside us.

It is no wonder that so many people today feel an emptiness that cannot be satisfied. The harder we try to achieve for ourselves, the more frustrated and unfulfilled we are. The more we get full of ourselves, the more empty we become. Only Christ can give us the richness of life that we desire. Only by being in a relationship with Him can we truly experience the richness of life. When your home is with Christ the more empty yourself, the fuller you become. The more you meet the needs of others, the more satisfaction you receive.

We all struggle trying desperately to determine what the reason for life is. What is the meaning of life, where is the fullness? Our goal should not be the pursuit of happiness, but instead the pursuit of a relationship with Christ. His richness alone will give you the fullness and peace that we all search for. Being a Christian is more than appearance, it is about commitment and relationship. It is about an intimacy with Christ that changes your thinking, attitudes, and priorities. It is about reliance, trust, and obedience. It is about Christ and His promises. May He find a home with you.

"The house of the wicked shall be destroyed,
The tent of honest men will stand firm."

PROVERBS 14:11

SOMETHING DIFFERENT

"What the Spirit brings is very different; love, joy, peace, patience, kindness, goodness, trustfulness, gentleness and self-control. There can be no law against things like that, of course."

GALATIANS 5:22-23

Doesn't it seem like there is a law for everything? We litigate and sue as a first course of action as we try to mandate certain behaviors. A world that is pushing God away looks to rules and regulations to try to find justice. Where has it gotten us?

The world needs an abundance of the fruits of the Spirit mentioned in this verse. The heart of a person full of the Spirit does not need a law to force them to love. Joy cannot be contained in a government policy. Peace and patience come from a place of security in Christ, not an armed force on a border. Kindness and goodness are at the heart of compassion, which is constantly challenged in our "me first" society. Truthfulness is a character trait that is in short supply in a world that cannot accept the absolute truth of the grace and mercy of God. Gentleness and self-control are concepts that have lost their importance in a media that glorifies the extreme and the violent. The path without the Spirit is a path that leads to nowhere. The Spirit is something different.

A real challenge for the believer is how to incorporate all these fruits of the Spirit into our daily lives. We too often give power and attention to the wrong path, forgetting our priority of love found in the Spirit. We must ask ourselves if our lives can be characterized by our real faith in Christ. Full of the Spirit, we can rely on Christ for true peace, joy, and patience. We can live our lives free from laws and full of kindness and goodness. We can be measured by the level of our gentleness and self-control when we are stressed. Above all we can love at all times when the Spirit dwells within us. We are free to love abundantly in Christ. Be different from the world. Let that difference be the Spirit of Christ living visibly and compassionately in all that you do.

"The fruit I give is better than gold, even the finest,
The return I make is better than pure silver."

PROVERBS 8:19

THE WORD OF GOD

"The Word of God is something alive and active: it cuts like a double-edged sword but more finely: it can slip through the place where the soul is divided from the spirit, or joints from the marrow; it can judge the secret emotions and thoughts. No created thing can hide from him; everything is uncovered and open to the eyes of the one to whom we must give account of ourselves."

HEBREWS 4:12-13

Your entire life is an open book to God. Every thought, emotion, and action stands before Him. This verse simultaneously gives great comfort and a warning. The assurance that God is alive and active assures us that God is interested in every facet of our lives. He finds and examines not only our actions, but also our soul. He knows the real you, the one that you think only you know.

We think we can hide things and that thoughts kept secret have no consequence. Nothing can be hidden; nothing can be kept secret from God. He knows the level of your commitment to Him. He peers into your soul, understanding your motives. He understands our emotions and knows how our thoughts affect our attitudes.

The Word of God serves so many purposes in the life of a Christian. It divides us from worldly attitudes, setting us apart to have our souls filled to the brim with the goodness of God. We have been given much, and God expects us to be accountable for how we use His gifts. It is a pure heart with pure motives and emotions that God desires. How will your accounting be to God? When you go before God, the one who knows your heart, will you be able to make a good accounting? Only God knows you completely. We are made up of more than what those around us see.

You cannot fool God. Let the Word of God fill you, taking control of your motives, thoughts, and emotions. God can see further into yourself than even you can. Let this blessing encompass you and let your body and soul be a place for the Word of God to be active and alive. Through you, the Holy Spirit and the Word is alive and touches the lives of others. Let your life be a home for the Word of God.

"A man's pride brings him humiliation,
he who humbles himself will win honor."

PROVERBS 29:23

LOVE PERFECTED

"Love will come to its perfection in us when we can face the day of Judgement without fear; because even in this world we have become as He is."

1 JOHN 4:17

Wouldn't it be wonderful to live in a world without fear? It seems like we all are constantly under some type of worldly threat. We could all probably make a long list of what we perceive as threats to our future: finances, health, job pressures, family pressures, safety, and peace. The list is inexhaustible.

So what are you really afraid of and why? When we cover ourselves in the love of God, our fears can be put in perspective. Above every fear and every threat we can know for sure, without doubt, that we are loved. We are loved as we are, now and forever. We are loved despite our sins, despite our selfishness, and despite our imperfection. God is that big and that forgiving. The best part is that His forgiveness is ours for the believing. The love of Christ has changed everything and our faith in Him allows us to live without fear. We live free, alive, and forgiven through faith. This world cannot overpower the love of God.

We have an easy solution as we try to respond to the love of God. We should love. Even in this world that works so hard to make itself important, we know that by mirroring the love of Christ we can choose Him first. We all want to be free, but it is through the love of Christ that we are truly free. No person wants to live in fear, and we do not have to when we trust the love of God. No one wants to wonder about their eternity, and that is unnecessary because of Christ.

In Him, love is fearless. In Him, love is freedom. In Him, love is eternal.

Let the love of God overpower your fears and rest in His compassion. Do not let the focus on worldly challenges separate you from the trust that God's love is eternal. He loves you at this exact moment and will never stop. Love others at this exact moment and never stop. It is then that love will find its perfection.

"Man's spirit is the lamp of God,
Searching his deepest self."

PROVERBS 20:27

WHAT DO YOU THINK ABOUT?

"Let your thoughts be on heavenly things,
not on the things that are on this earth..."

COLOSSIANS 3:3

What is really important? If you put your thoughts today in order, where would God rate? We are continually bombarded with every distraction and anxiety of the world, while continually looking away from the One, the only One, which can make sense of it all. Do you think a politician will solve your problems? They won't. Will the government find the solutions to your everyday life? It can't. Can a raise or promotion make things easy? It never will. Diets and self-help methods assure you they can make you happy. They will always fail you. Do not be fooled. A bigger house, a fat bank account, and a flashy car will not increase your joy.

The peace that passes all understanding comes from only one source, Almighty God. Filling our minds with earthly things pushes us further away from where we are encouraged to focus...heavenly things. We are all in this life for the long haul, the eternal vision. Surely, we deal with day-to-day stress and events, but we can never lose sight of God and never forget that temporary events should never get in the way of our faith in Christ. Through Him, you are already equipped, already able, and most importantly already loved into eternity. Day-to-day challenges too often lead us to think that we or others around us are the solution. We tend to look inward, instead of upward for solutions and peace. The search for answers should start with God.

It can be a helpless feeling when we feel completely out of control, but that is exactly where a Christian should find peace. The Bible tells us about the problems that man faces when we try to replace God and put ourselves above Him. Alone we are broken. In Him we are healed. Alone we are anxious. Jesus gives us peace. Alone we are lonely. God showers us with His presence.

What impact would it have on your life if you concentrated every day on love, peace, unity, compassion, and sacrifice instead of listening to the minute-by-minute news broadcasts? What would happen if you concentrated on investing in the lives of others instead of the stock market? This world will always fail. Our God has already won. What will you think about today?

"Fear of God gives good grounds for confidence,
In Him, His children find a refuge."

PROVERBS 14:26

PSALM 27

Verses 1

Verses 13-14

"God is my light and my salvation,
Who need I fear?
God is the fortress of my life
Of whom should I be afraid?"
"This I believe: I shall see the goodness of God,
In the land of the living.
Put your hope in God, be strong, let your heart be bold,
put your hope in God."

MY PERSPECTIVES

MY PERSPECTIVES

MY PERSPECTIVES

MY PERSPECTIVES

MY PERSPECTIVES

CPSIA information can be obtained
at www.ICGtesting.com
Printed in the USA
LVHW092320051221
705374LV00002B/63